ACADEMIC FREEDOM

ACADEMIC FREEDOM

Conrad Russell

London and New York

First published 1993
by Routledge
11 New Fetter Lane, London EC4P 4EE

Simultaneously published in the USA and Canada
by Routledge
29 West 35th Street, New York, NY 10001

Typeset in 10 on 12 point Garamond by
Computerset, Harmondsworth, Middlesex
Printed in Great Britain by T.J. Press (Padstow) Ltd, Padstow, Cornwall

British Library Cataloguing in Publication Data
Russell, Conrad
Academic Freedom
I. Title
378.1

Library of Congress Cataloging in Publication Data
Russell, Conrad
Academic Freedom / Conrad Russell.
p. cm.
Includes bibliographical references and index.
1. Academic freedom – Great Britain. 2. Higher education and state – Great
Britain. 3. University autonomy – Great Britain.
I. Title.
LC72.5.G7R87 1993
378.1'21—dc20
92–30810

ISBN 0-415-03714-X 0-415-03715-8 (pbk)

The freedom within the law to question and test received wisdom, and to put forward new ideas and controversial or unpopular opinions without placing themselves in jeopardy of losing their jobs or privileges they may have at their institutions.

(Academic Freedom amendment to Education Reform Bill,
moved by Lord Jenkins of Hillhead, 19 May 1988)

There is an obvious tension between the public funding of Higher Education institutions and the need to preserve their essential autonomy.

(Lord Mackay of Clashfern, Lord Chancellor,
House of Lords Official Report, 19 April 1988, col. 1365)

CONTENTS

PREFACE

This book was commissioned as a result of the clash between Government and Universities during the Education Reform Bill of 1988. I went into those debates, as a brand new member of the House of Lords, singing the battle hymn of the republic of learning. I was engaged in arguing a passionate single-issue defence of my own profession. Since then, as an active member of the House of Lords, and of the Liberal Democrat Party, I have acquired a foot in both camps. That fact, together with the academic discipline of trying to understand one's opponents' point of view, has produced a very different book from the one I would have written in 1988. Those who listen will still hear the battle hymn, but they will hear other tunes too. In particular, the book has been informed by a growing and painful awareness of the very limited amount of money a government could spend if it chose.

The book which has emerged is intended as a contribution to the task of working out new terms of cooperation between the Universities and the State. It is, no doubt, a contribution from one side of the fence, and will be seen among politicians as that. Yet, in any negotiation, the spelling out of opening positions must be a statement of one side's point of view, however much it may be informed by attempts to understand the rival viewpoint. It is intended as a contribution to a dialogue, not as a series of ultimate answers. The departure of Lady Thatcher, between whom and the Universities there existed a passionate mutual hostility, has made such a dialogue possible, but it has not yet made it take place. The temperature may have fallen, but in 1991, there does not seem to me to be on either side any more understanding of the views of the other than there was in 1988. If dialogue is now possible, attempts should be made to begin it. Much of this book is inevitably written with reference to the present Government, led by John Major, and holding assumptions inherited from the reign of Margaret Thatcher.

It would be dangerously easy for academics to overestimate the amount the accession of a new Government could change. Part of the reason for this is that the root of many of the assumptions here disputed is inherent in the nature of the State as at present constituted. Many of them, and especially those which start from the Treasury's search for accountability, are rooted in Whitehall rather than Westminster, and therefore are not susceptible to change by General Elections. It is also inherent in the profession of politics that those who practise it are liable to find their eyes are bigger than their stomachs: they want to do more than they can afford to pay for. No General Election is ever likely to change that. Above all, no new Government, of whatever party, will find that its accession creates a penny more money in the country as a whole. Any Government more successful in its economic policy than its predecessor would find that success took a long time. For these reasons, many of the questions here discussed will be likely to remain as live under any future Government as they are today.

In writing this book, I have inevitably been influenced by many overlapping loyalties, but the book expresses a personal view, and nothing more nor less. Though I hope many colleagues will agree with many things in it, I doubt whether any will agree with them all, and some will disagree with many. Nor is this book in any sense written on behalf of my party. I have of course been influenced by many ideas derived from my party, but in no sense can this book be seen as an expression of party policy. My political, like my professional, colleagues may well disagree with very large parts of it. The area in which party influence on me is strongest is the discussion of those issues of accountability which affect the Universities equally with other public services. This is an area where there is a great deal of thinking still to be done. This book aims to make only a small preliminary contribution to that thinking. I hope fellow members of my party may feel that my views on this issue are in line with party philosophy, but they make no attempt to represent party policy: they are a personal view only.

The same applies to other associations and institutions to which I belong or owe loyalty. I write as a member of King's College, London, of the Institute of Historical Research in the University of London, of the Campaign for Academic Autonomy and of the Association of University Teachers. I have been influenced by loyalties to, and conversations within, all these bodies, and also by the impressive briefing of the Committee of Vice-Chancellors and Principals. I hope this book contains many passages in which members of these bodies may feel I am speaking for them, but I am also certain that it contains many in which they will not. A view influenced by so many overlapping loyalties must inevitably be a personal one.

This book has also benefitted immensely from conversation with many colleagues both academic and political. It has been stimulated by the contributions of many who spoke on both sides in the House of Lords debates in 1988, and by personal conversations with more people than I can hope to name. It is without wishing to minimize my debt to any of the others that I would like to thank Rowland Eustace, Brian Flowers, Robert Jackson, Bob Moore, Mary Morgan, John Roberts, Nancy Seear, Antony Smith, David Starkey and Michael Thompson. The multifariousness of this list should be obvious enough to show that they are not responsible for any views here expressed.

As always, my greatest debt is to my wife. As a historian of the University of Oxford, she has helped to give me perspective on this subject. She has been apt to tell me, in my moments of deepest depression, that it was worse in 1547 or in 1647. In doing so, she has helped me to keep my faith in the power of the Universities to survive the onslaught on them. In addition to the historical perspective, she has always helped me to preserve an external perspective. In my moments of greatest passion, she has always forced on my attention the valid points in the opposing point of view, and in particular, has helped to preserve me from falling victim to the popular and academic myth of the inexhaustible public purse. This dual contribution has added greatly to the intellectual rigour of the book. For the numerous faults, weaknesses and gaps which remain, I alone am responsible. If writing this book has persuaded me of any one thing, it is that no single person will ever be capable of solving the problems it addresses.

Conrad Russell
September 1991

INTRODUCTION

The words 'academic freedom' have often caused confusion because they come from a medieval intellectual tradition which pre-dates most of the current meanings of the word 'freedom'. It is the contention of this book that much of that intellectual tradition is still valid, and as desperately needed for defence against John Major as it ever was against John Lackland. Because Universities were originally seen as quasi-ecclesiastical institutions, the claims of Universities to academic freedom have always been rooted in an intellectual tradition created to defend the autonomy of the medieval Church. In the translation from that tradition into modern idiom, vital shades of meaning are sometimes lost.

The City of Lucca, the last of the Italian city states to preserve its autonomy, used to take great pride in this fact. Its pride was embodied in the town motto, *'libertas'*, which was inscribed over all the gates of the town. This motto said nothing about the distribution of power within Lucca: it recorded the town's independence from the outside world. It embodied an ideal of liberty whose essential expression was a claim to sovereignty. One night in 1797, a group of young men went round the town with chisels, and altered all these inscriptions to *'libertà'*. This translation into a modern vernacular was at once seen by the town, when it woke, as a declaration of allegiance to the French Revolution.[1]

The ideal of academic freedom is often misunderstood because, in a modern world, it is forced to defend the first of these ideals in the language of the second. The Academic Freedom amendment to the Education Bill of 1988, proposed by Lord Jenkins of Hillhead, claimed for academics:

the freedom within the law to question and test received wisdom, and to put forward new ideas and controversial or unpopular

1

opinions without placing themselves in jeopardy of losing their jobs or privileges they may have at their institutions.

This wording was cast in entirely post-French Revolutionary language, and in terms of an ideal of freedom of speech which descends straight from Mill's *Essay on Liberty*.[2] Yet behind this very modern claim are echoes, which any academic is attuned to hear, of a very much older tradition which guaranteed the autonomy of the medieval Church. For any academic, there is a tendency to assume that their rights to free speech are inextricably intertwined with their right to run their own affairs. The history of Lord Jenkins' office, as Chancellor of Oxford University, illustrates this point very well. In proposing this amendment, he was behaving in a way his predecessors, from the thirteenth century onwards, would have instantly understood.

The medieval Church, too, wanted freedom to put forward controversial or unpopular opinions, and its claims to liberties were always designed to defend its freedom to state spiritual values which temporal rulers, from time to time, might find profoundly irksome. The Church was always aware of the danger the irritation of the State might pose to its spiritual freedom. The decrees of the synod of Ingelheim, in 948, for example, enact that: 'the holy synod be not harassed or interrupted by any assault of laymen'.[3] Popes Gregory VII and Boniface VIII, because they had annoyed temporal powers, ended their lives in military captivity. Archbishop Thomas Becket was not so fortunate. For that reason, the claims of the medieval Church to freedom to discharge its own spiritual functions were always treated as inseparable from its claims to jurisdictional autonomy. So great a power of ideas, facing so great a power of the sword, could only survive if it established a very firm taboo on State interference in its own affairs in any shape or form. The Church, then, believed it could only preserve its liberty by preserving its liberties.

Academics, because their privileges were originally ecclesiastical and guaranteed by the Pope, are in this the lineal heirs of the medieval Church. In twentieth-century Britain, they are also in a very similar practical situation to that of the medieval Church. They enjoy an intellectual power and prestige which may often appear to those who feel ill at ease with it to be overwhelming. The sort of populism for which Mr Kenneth Clarke has spoken is often born out of an intense resentment of academic sense of superiority, and is thus the lineal descendant of medieval anti-clericalism. Yet at the same time, the academic is aware of his overwhelming dependence on the outside world to support him – a dependence he shares with the medieval

Church before him. While the populist feels insufferably patronized, the academic may at the same time feel a Woody Allen sense of helplessness in the face of a mighty outside world over which he has no physical control. Both reactions are not without excuse, yet those who hold them are usually quite unable to understand each other. When they meet at close quarters, they may give rise to a conflict made bitter by incomprehension. In this too, academics are the heirs of the medieval Church. It is no wonder, then, that in their relations with the State, they have inherited much the same potential for conflict which affected the medieval Church. The current assault by the State on the Universities is thus in a long tradition. Yet within that tradition, it is an assault to which there are few parallels, because it is designed to change all the values by which Universities operate. Perhaps only a clergyman who had lived through the reign of Henry VIII would be capable of understanding how the Universities now feel. On the frustrations felt by the State, I am not competent to speak.

It is in this situation that it has become necessary to reassert the medieval ideal of liberties, to argue that Universities have their own independent sphere of judgement, in which the State should not meddle. The argument runs that it is only by this sort of autonomy to govern their own affairs that academics may protect a world in which they are free to exercise their basic rights of freedom of speech and of thought. It is not enough to defend these by the law of the State alone, when the State may, perhaps entirely unwittingly, take away conditions in which these rights can be exercised. The opinion that government is devaluing the standards of the University degree, for example, enjoys only a nugatory freedom if it can only be asserted by spitting in the wind, against opponents who enjoy overwhelming physical and financial power. The standards of the University degree, and many other things also, can only ever be defended effectively if they are recognized as purely academic matters, in which the State can have no legitimate say. It is only by defending a medieval liberty, a sphere of academic freedom in which the State does not enter, that academic freedom in a Millite sense can ever be effectively defended. If the state cannot accept this, Universities should not continue to exist, for they will serve no useful purpose save that of rubber-stamping decisions reached in ignorance by the State. Whether the State wants Universities on these terms is a question for it to decide. What it must understand before taking the decision is that it is these terms or none: there can be no others. The State has hitherto decided, often with some reluctance, that the answer to this question is 'Yes'.

The medieval idea of a 'liberty', into which the State does not enter, is a very old one indeed, and we are sometimes told that it was rendered obsolete by Thomas Cromwell in the reign of Henry VIII. In relation to the Church, this may possibly be so, though the question is more complex than is sometimes supposed. Even the most cursory study of defences of the privileges of the Universities, however, must show that whatever the Church may have done, Universities have kept this ideal alive into modern times. It is now, perhaps, an ideal old enough for its time to have come again, for it is capable of merging with the new political pluralism which has grown out of the issue of devolution.

It is widely perceived as unjust that Scotland should be governed by a party which won only 25 per cent of the vote there, and it is argued that the Government's authority can be accepted only in return for a very large degree of local autonomy. Are Universities, where the victorious party won only 14 per cent of the vote, entitled to any benefit from the same argument?[4] Before this argument is dismissed out of hand, it is worth remembering that the City, with more power but no more right, *has* exercised an effective veto over the election of a government to which it could not consent. It is difficult to argue that this can, or even should, be otherwise: a country needs money, and money, in an increasingly international world, cannot be impounded at the Customs and forbidden to leave the country. Yet it must be admitted that such a veto carries with it an implied threat to democracy.

To argue for the extending of the power enjoyed by the City to all professions and regions would be a proto-anarchist *reductio ad absurdum*. Yet at the same time it must be admitted that government by consent is a very tender plant, and we uproot it at our peril. For all of us, there is a point beyond which we simply become unable to give consent, and Governments push us beyond that point at their own risk: academics, like money, must remain free to leave the country. It should, perhaps, be regarded as a maxim of Government that people should not normally be pushed beyond the limits of their consent. Doctors, for example, have the Hippocratic Oath, and it is to be hoped, if Government were to require them to do things which contradict that oath, that they would refuse their consent. They would certainly be poor doctors if they did not. Academics have no formal equivalent of the Hippocratic Oath, yet they too have professional values, and are no use to society if they give them up. To make an academic devalue the standard of his degree, while requiring him to swear in public that he is doing no such thing, is perhaps the equivalent of requiring a doctor to violate his

Hippocratic Oath, and that is the requirement academics face at present.

It is clearly impossible for every profession to elect a separate government: there must be one Government for us all. That being so, it is perhaps essential for a Government to return towards a medieval ideal of 'liberties': it should recognize spheres of independent professional judgement, within which it is incompetent to meddle. In dealing with groups of its subjects, just as in dealing with the internal affairs of families, governments should perhaps accept an ideal equivalent to Article 2 of the UN Charter, which forbids governments to meddle in the internal affairs of member states. Like Article 2 itself, such a rule could not be absolute or incapable of exception. Yet, just as it is only possible to have a United Nations if such a rule is accepted as normal practice, it is perhaps only possible to have a government if it accepts such a restraint except when there is an overwhelming national interest to the contrary. If learned professions are not to enjoy a degree of autonomy, either the professions or Government by consent must in due course disappear.

For most of the early twentieth century, this debate appeared to be an exhausted volcano, and relations between Universities and the State were more amicable than they have been for most of their history. For the State, and above all for the voters, Universities were valuable as a means of social advancement, and therefore as a means for the peaceful dismantling of a hereditary class system. For academics, the rapidly increasing amount of money flowing from the coffers of the State made it possible for them to adjust even to changes as massive as the expansion involved in the Robbins Report of 1963.[5] The relationship appeared to meet Adam Smith's classic criterion for a bargain: it was in the interests of both sides.

There was little sign of any other storm liable to blow cooperation away. The breakdown of the English class structure since 1945 has been proceeding slowly and comparatively peacefully. It has certainly never generated tensions similar to those produced by the breakdown of racial segregation in the United States. England has never developed a 'politically correct' movement because it has never had need of one. It has not, since Catholic Emancipation, had to attempt anything as difficult as the United States' acceptance of the equal rights of Black Americans. There has been no foreign war in which undergraduates were called upon to fight, and therefore no head-on clash of values in that area between Universities and the State. We have had no Vietnam. There is no British Bible Belt, and even in Northern Ireland, there has been no demand for the teaching of creation science, and no continuing clash between the values of Universities and those of society around them. The permissive revolution of the 1960s perhaps disturbed the equanimity of Universities more than most other social changes, but this too, thanks in part to the wisdom of Roy Jenkins and David Steel, went through in Britain with a great deal less conflict than in some other countries. Oxford Common Rooms might be dismayed by undergraduates' insistence on a right to be *known* to have their girlfriends in College all night, but since a blind eye had always been turned to this phenomenon, an insistence that the eye be opened usually caused no more than mild pain. It undoubtedly helped that this period saw a larger number of junior appointments than any other since the war. This prevented clashes about permissiveness from taking a staff-versus-student form. Moreover, the private morals of undergraduates were never any threat to the essential operations of Universities, and posed no problem for academic freedom. Perhaps only assaults on freedom of speech had the potential to create a serious clash between Universities and the State, and here the values of the State were so widely shared inside Universities themselves that the potential for a clash was not very great. Indeed, the vast majority of the academic community was able to draw courage from its agreement with the State. This issue illustrates the way in which the power of the State in British Universities inhibits the growth of any serious threat to academic freedom from within Universities themselves. This is not only because the State may intervene to defend academic freedom, though there are times when we have been glad enough to deploy that argument against intolerant undergraduates or colleagues. It is also because the total financial dependence of British Universities on the State has always created a weather eye to any threat to academic freedom coming from the State. The desire to defend academic freedom because the State might otherwise infringe it has been a powerful inhibiting force on any movement against academic freedom originating with the Universities.

This period of peace came to an end because of the shortage of public money created by the oil crises of 1973 and 1979. There had been doubts, ever since the 1960s, how far the expansion planned by the Robbins Report could be carried through without threatening the quality of the traditional University. The Thatcher Government had to tackle this problem, but instead of firmly resolving it in favour either of quantity or of quality, and trying to carry the academic community with it in whichever choice it reached, it decided that the problem could be made to go away by the remorseless pursuit of 'efficiency', meaning a steady reduction in the costs per student, which we were told was meant to produce the same quality for less money. This attempt merged with the Government's desire to see professions as trade unions to be controlled. It was in pursuit of this policy that the 1988 Education Act introduced a vast new machinery designed to make Universities more 'accountable' for the public money they received. This Act set up an apparatus for Whitehall intervention in what had always previously been seen as matters of academic judgement. It was in reply to that interventionist urge that the cry of 'academic freedom' was first raised. The Academic Freedom amendment to the 1988 bill was moved by Lord Jenkins of Hillhead, Chancellor of Oxford University. It was carried against the Government in a division in the House of Lords, and has remained in the Act. Because it was necessary to win a majority for that amendment, it claimed less than many academics would have liked. It has served, though, as a benchmark for a great deal of subsequent debate on the issue of academic freedom. This has become so bitter that in a University community which used throughout the 1960s and 1970s to be politically divided in very much the same proportions as the rest of the country, support for the Conservatives has fallen to 17 per cent in the election of 1987, and to 14 per cent in the election of 1992. Perhaps never since the victorious Parliamentary Visitors entered Oxford in 1647 to enforce the rule of the victors in the English Civil War, have we had a regime so alienated from its Universities.

In all this debate, the issue of public money has been paramount. To the Government, it has appeared as a claim by academics to freedom to squander public money in any way they choose, without saying what they have done with it. To academics, it has appeared to be an attempt to cheapen their operation (in both senses of the term) to a point which was incompatible with freedom in academic judgement, and liable to destroy the very essence of their operations. This debate has now raged continuously for some five years, and almost no progress towards mutual understanding has yet been made.

It was always likely that in Britain any conflict over academic freedom would arise from the State's control over the power of the purse. The almost total dependence of British Universities on the State for the funding of their basic operations has for a long time left them dangerously vulnerable to the power of the State. Conversely, the amount of money the State has put into the Universities since the Robbins Report was so great that the Treasury, the most powerful institution in Britain, was always likely to attempt to control it more strictly. For a long time, some academics, such as Lord Beloff, founder of the independent

University of Buckingham, had seen that Universities' dependence on the State was dangerously great. The fault was always visible, and the earthquake could be predicted. It is not surprising that relations between Universities and the State have broken down. It is not a matter of dispute that the dependence was unhealthy. What was, and is, in doubt is whether any alternative exists.

Universities and the State need each other precisely because their values and priorities are so different from each other. Each depends on the other for those things which its professional discipline and code of values makes it least able to understand. Perhaps, then, it is not surprising that reactions between Universities and their States have tended to be fraught with tension and misunderstanding. In England, bitter quarrels between the two can be traced back at least to 1209.

Yet what is striking is not just how regularly there have been quarrels, but how regularly they have been successfully made up. Periods of bitter conflict have consistently alternated with periods of intense mutual congratulation. Just as the periods of tension have never been without the underlying capacity for goodwill, so the periods of goodwill have never been without an underlying tension. The relationship is perhaps more like a stormy but vital marriage than any other model to which it can be compared.

Academics, like the Church, from which their profession descends, are supposed to pursue an other-worldly ideal while depending on others for their sources of income. This, as the clergy have learnt very well, is an inherently fraught relationship. Demands for autonomy on the one hand compete with all the familiar paraphernalia of anti-clericalism on the other. Stories of academics junketing at conferences on public money are the lineal descendants of all those Reformation stories which accused Catholic priests of using the Confessional for the purpose of seduction. The benefactor's sense that he is being taken for a ride is always likely to come into conflict with the recipient's sense that he is being dictated to. Since academics, like the clergy, are no better than other men and women, and are equipped with all the same collection of human failings, and since those who pay the piper are always tempted to call the tune even if they are tone-deaf, both sides' potential sense of ill-usage has always had something to feed on.

Yet, since bad news grows in the telling, mythology on both sides has probably always outstripped fact. It is doubtful whether Thomas Cromwell's monastic visitors in the reign of Henry VIII actually left leaves from defaced manuscripts of Duns Scotus blowing in the wind in New College Quad. At the same time, it is doubtful whether late

eighteenth-century Oxford was really as sleepy and intellectually de-
funct as it appeared to Jeremy Bentham. Bentham, like other young men
with something new to offer, tended to despise those who came before
him, yet both Oxford and Blackstone have survived his contempt. The
Parliamentary Visitors of 1647 were not necessarily enemies of all
scholarship: they included John Selden, one of the greatest scholars of
his age, whose name now appears on the Bodleian Library benefactors'
Roll. Similarly, Oxford in the 1950s was never as full of stupid public-
school oarsmen as many people believed it to be. The philistine
dictatorial State and the fraudulent and idle University, like the faithless
wife and the roving husband, both grow in the telling.

Yet, when all allowance is made for this tendency, the disputes
between the State and the Universities which boiled up around the
Education Reform Bill of 1988 deserve to be regarded as among the half-
dozen great quarrels between Universities and the State in our national
history. In the years since then, both sides have retreated warily from
confrontation, yet there is no sign that the gap in understanding which
then opened up has been in any way closed. It was those debates which
led to the commissioning of this book, and while the passage of time
since then has cooled some of the heat, it has perhaps also made it easier
to try to reopen some of the telephone lines.

This book, because it is the work of a serving academic, is necessarily
written from one side of that divide. Yet it is also the work of one who,
since 1988, has come to have a foot in both the academic and political
camps, and who may therefore hope to be able occasionally to interpret
one side to the other. The common fate of such attempts is of course
execration from both. Had this book been written in 1988, it would of
course have met such a fate, and may yet do so. Yet it is also in the nature
of this book that it could not have been written in 1988: the passage of
time has conferred some sense, which the heat of battle did not permit,
of what the other side was driving at. This book cannot pretend to be
truly balanced, yet it is less unbalanced that it would have been if written
in the heat of the moment. If the same is true of the response, it might yet
contribute to healing a breach between two parties whose need for each
other is not going to go away.

In the 1988 debates, each side was asserting a valid ideal, but neither
could see why the other believed its ideal was threatened. As a consequence, there was a tendency for the two sides to talk past each other.
This phenomenon is of course normal in parliamentary debate, and
what is perhaps unusual about this occasion, and marks it out as a
debate of some quality, is that attempts to reach understanding are still

quietly in progress three years later. Not many parliamentary debates leave so much grit in so many oysters.

The academic ideal, encapsulated in the Academic Freedom amendment, was that of free enquiry. Over and over again, academics asserted the necessity to Universities, and the value to the country of allowing academic enquiry to be directed to the pursuit of knowledge for its own sake, regardless of any fear of dismissal, need to conform to Government contracts, to fill out forms, or to kowtow to any fashionable creed of the day. The sense that this idea was under threat shows through almost every academic speech made in the course of the debates. It is, of course, an ideal as old as Socrates, and doubtless older, but the sense that it needed reassertion and defence against its enemies roused an academic reaction in favour of autonomy perhaps stronger than any which has happened since the Parliamentary Visitors came to Oxford in 1647.

The Government, while not disputing this case in principle, did not understand why it appeared to others to be at issue. Their concern was with asserting another principle, equally universally accepted, that of accountability for public money. Like the academics, they could not understand why their case was not instantly accepted. The Lord Chancellor said: 'surely it cannot be argued that the Government, on the taxpayers' behalf, have no right to determine how these substantial sums are disbursed?'.[6] This is the age-old principle of paying the piper and calling the tune.

Any serious discussion must begin from the recognition that this is a clash between two valid principles. The case for free academic enquiry must be unanswerable, for without it, what is the value in having academics at all? Yet at the same time, the principle that public money ought to be accounted for is at the heart of democratic principles. Taxes are voted by consent, and that consent must rest on some understanding about how they are to be used. Consent apart, the urge to corruption goes back to the days when Achan hid the spoils of Jericho, and no category of the human race can claim a holiness so great as to make it immune. Any right to receive public money must carry with it a reciprocal duty, and where there is a duty, there must be accountability for its performance.

Neither academics nor indeed anyone else has a natural right to receive public money. Over the past 50 years, the language of entitlement has been used, and indeed rightly used, to broaden the social base of access to higher education, medicine, social services, the law and a great deal else. Because the language of entitlement has been used, it has been dangerously easy to think in terms of a natural right to education, medical treatment, and a great deal else. Under our system of government, rights are not legally natural, but conferred by statute and common law: they are contingent. The system of law apart, the enjoyment of any rights, whether natural or otherwise, must to a degree be contingent on the ability of someone to pay for them. Were it to be established to the general satisfaction that everyone had a natural right to a university education, the amount of money in the country simply would not stretch to making that right effective. In fact, as far as I can see, no one has a *right* to a University education: if they have a University education, it is because it is recognized as in the national interest that they should. Though this Government in fact drew back before Clive Jenkins' warning that it might prove to be the first Government to close a University since Idi Amin, the right of a sovereign Parliament to close a University must exist, however inexpedient it may be to exercise it. Indeed, there is no external compulsion on the Government to have any Universities at all: they will do so, if they do, only because they recognize some benefit which follows from it. Under these circumstances, it is hard to argue against the principle of accountability for public money.

Yet there is a point where the demand for accountability becomes, in the literal and not the legal sense, *ultra vires*: it is beyond their powers. Accountability must not be extended to the point where it interferes with the proper discharge of the service for which money was granted. When I was a boy, I had a neighbour whose walls were decorated with First World War cartoons. I particularly remember one which showed a dugout, shaking at the blast of exploding shells. The frightened soldier inside was picking up a field telephone which was exclaiming: 'Colonel Fitz-Shrapnel orders you to indent *immediately* for the seventeen jars of raspberry jam issued to you on the 15th *ult*!' The recipient's expletives were deleted. At this point, accountability interferes with the proper discharge of duties. There is also a point where demands for accountability run up against the limits of competence. That a fighter pilot is accountable for the use of his plane is only proper: he cannot use it to pop over to Paris to see his girlfriend. Yet if he is to be held accountable for the detailed use of his controls, for choice of speed, altitude and angle of approach to landing, this must be done, if at all, only by a fellow pilot: Government lacks the competence to do it. If, for example, it instructs him to fly at a particular speed in order to save fuel, it may unwittingly risk hazarding his plane, and the order may well be disobeyed.

The conflict between freedom and accountability is usually a clash between right and right. Clashes between right and right usually resolve themselves into boundary problems, in which the sphere of one principle must be distinguished from the sphere of another. When the border becomes ambiguous or obscure, guerilla war may break out all the way along it. This is very much the present state of relations between Government and the academic community. Under these circumstances, an attempt to re-survey the boundaries may perhaps be useful.

It is perhaps natural, at a time when relations between the State and Universities have been so fraught, that there should be voices on both sides hankering after divorce, or at least a degree of judicial separation. Pressure on Universities to recruit high-fee overseas students, and to sell their services for contract research, marks Government willingness to see them finance some part of their services from sources other than the Exchequer. At the same time, voices among Vice-Chancellors have been heard exploring the possibility of a top-up fee from home students, thus conferring on Universities a control over their marginal income. Both voices express the familiar conviction that the grass is greener in the next field.

A divorce between Universities and the State is a legal possibility. Universities are private corporations, and are under no legal obligation to take in any British students at all. It is of course true that public funding is provided on the understanding that they should take in well-qualified UK applicants.[7] However, Universities are under no compulsion to accept the public funding, and should it consistently fail to match the cost of the operations they are asked to undertake in return for it, they could find themselves under overwhelming pressure to refuse it. Universities, in fact, are by law, private corporations, and therefore are under no more obligation than any other private business to operate at a loss. It is, then, possible to imagine a situation in which British Universities refuse to take in British students at the rate at which Government is prepared to pay for them. The Government agrees that there is no legal obstacle to this course. They would then be left free to take in as many high-fee overseas students as they could recruit, and to undertake contract research for foreign buyers. While it is possible to imagine a situation in which this possibility is less unattractive than any alternative, it would be wrong to delude ourselves that it is an attractive possibility. Some experience of the market for overseas students would suggest that it would about suffice to keep up Oxford and Cambridge as genuine Universities, and would leave the rest to go to the wall.

What we should not delude ourselves into believing is that the British economy will support any substantial number of private Universities financed by fee-paying students. It has been the experience of the University of Buckingham that it has depended heavily on recruitment of overseas students. The national absence of state-funded places would of course increase the number of British students willing and able to pay full-cost fees, but it is unlikely that it would become large. This is in part the result of the capital-intensive character of University education. The cost of scientific equipment, and the cost of a good library both increase at a far more rapid rate than the Retail Price Index. This is not a peculiarity of British Universities: American College fees, determined in a system with a much larger element of the free market, have risen much faster through the 1980s than either British University costs or the Retail Price Index in either country. It is probably true in all subjects, though particularly visibly true in the sciences, that an education in yesterday's ideas is not worth paying for. It is therefore essential for a University which wishes to keep its degrees valuable to those who take them to keep up with changes in ideas, techniques, books and equipment in the subjects it teaches. Since academics all the way round the world learn from each other's ideas, this means that the growth of Universities has made the increases in their costs exponential. Moreover, Universities are a quality market, and in a quality market, it is the effect of competition to drive the price up and not down. The difference between the cost of a Yale or Harvard degree and that of a competent middle-rank private College may be only two or three thousand dollars a year. Yet, since the number of top jobs available to graduates is limited, and they will necessarily tend to go to those whose degrees are regarded as the best, the best quality degree will almost always be better value for money than the second best, even if it is also more expensive. To put the point bluntly, if George Bush had been a graduate of Trinity College, Hartford and not of Yale, he might not have reached the White House. Moreover, if his opponent in 1992 had not been a fellow Yalie, he might not have left it.

Private Universities flourish, if at all, in countries with high personal disposable income and a good deal of economic inequality. In those countries, there is a pool of rich capable of paying fees enough to finance a scholarship scheme capable of bringing in more able pupils from lower-income families. In Britain, which is still a country of fairly even income distribution, this pool of rich does not exist, and it would take a very long time to create it if it were regarded as desirable to do so. This is in part because of the very rapid increase in the cost of housing. In 1989, total household expenditure in Britain was £315 billion, of which £49.6 billion or 15.7 per cent went on housing. This figure now exceeds the £47.6 billion spent by the British on income tax. An even more surprising figure is the £57 billion, or 18.1 per cent, spent on transport and communication. This figure exceeds the total yield from VAT. The two figures together suggest that the British are spending a very high proportion indeed of their disposable income, either on housing, or on the cost of getting to work from a place where they can afford to live.[8] Moreover, since University costs represent a very heavy concentrated expenditure over a limited number of years, they are likely to involve borrowing, and, as everyone who has compared the price of his house with the actual cost of his mortgage over its total duration knows very well, the use of credit substantially increases the real cost to the buyer. Under these circumstances, it is not likely that the British could sustain a mass market in privately financed higher education. The effect of reliance on fees would be to restrict higher education to those sections of society which are both affluent and conditioned to thinking of it as the natural end of the adolescent *cursus honorum*. It is not necessary to labour the point that these will not always be the most able people. The effect of such a policy would be that the standards of our chemists and engineers, not to mention the standard of our lawyers and our school-teachers, would decline. There is no need to labour the point that this would not be in the national interest.

Both for these reasons, and because in a democratic society a demand for higher education must be listened to, it is no more likely that Governments will decide to dispense with Universities than it is that Universities will decide to dispense with Governments. Their mutual dependence is inescapable, and the contemplation of divorce will only postpone the urgently needed resort to marriage guidance. Government and Universities not for the first time, must learn to live with each other.

This book is addressed only to issues arising from Government policy on Universities. Some, but not all, of those issues are unique to Universities. Others, especially those involved with the issue of account-ability for public money, may be relevant to the management of other public services. It will be for others to say what the arguments of this book have to offer to general debate on the public services, and on the limits of the Government's useful role in a mixed economy.

1

THE IDEAL OF ACADEMIC FREEDOM

If even the Newtonian philosophy were not permitted to be questioned, mankind could not feel as complete assurance of its truth as they now do.

(J. S. Mill, *Essay on Liberty*)[1]

Anyone who does not wish to be circumvented or have his rights prejudiced should look to himself in future, and be sure that he does not go too far to accommodate these people of the University in the matter of granting commissions or other things. Observe the way in which they have begun to elevate themselves in a spirit of pride against the Bishop and church of Lincoln over the question of the Chancellor's commission and other things, saying that they can in no way be cited before the bishop outside the town of Oxford. In all these matters they have pleaded their alleged customs, liberties, privileges and statutes. Therefore it is necessary to proceed with care so as not to condescend to them too far.

(Registrar of the Bishop of Lincoln, 1290)[2]

The ideal of academic freedom, like the Church, has often appeared to its defenders to be in danger when those from whom the threat is alleged to come cannot see what all the fuss is about. This is because, from the very beginning of the history of Universities in the West, the claim to free intellectual enquiry and to control over their own teaching and degrees has been identified with the claim to the privileges of a self-governing corporation to run its own affairs. How far these two claims are necessarily interdependent is a question which has, perhaps, been insufficiently examined on both sides. That the University of Oxford should wish to control its own degrees and its own licences to teach was natural enough, but it was not self-evident to the Mayor of Oxford that this implied jurisdictional immunity for a student accused of murdering

15

his mistress. The resulting quarrel in effect closed down the University of Oxford for five years from 1209 to 1214. The 1214 settlement, under the auspices of the Papal Legate, was one of the earliest occasions on which the relationship between the University and the State was repaired and a new recognition of their interdependence built up. Since the University was claiming a jurisdictional autonomy which went with ecclesiastical status, the key figure at first was the local ecclesiastical diocesan authority, the Bishop of Lincoln. The result was a series of disputes between the University and the Bishop of Lincoln which were as bitter as many of the disputes with the State, though less likely to end in bloodshed than those with the town of Oxford.

The key figure in resolving these disputes came to be the Chancellor of the University, a figure with buffer status between the rival jurisdictions rather on the lines of the old University Grants Committee. He was a nominee of the Bishop of Lincoln, but in 1367, in a crucial concession, the Bishop conferred on the University the right to elect its Chancellor. He thus combined being chosen by the University with being appointed by the Bishop. He also combined these with powers conferred by the Crown, and thus had both civil and ecclesiastical jurisdiction. He was thus the point in which all theories of power, ecclesiastical and secular, ascending and descending, were blended. When troubled with summonses to appear outside the University, he rapidly developed a *pro forma* set of excuses, alleging an influx of students, the Fair of St Frideswide, trouble with the town and the preparation of a sermon.[3] Behind the University was the Pope, who gave a crucial confirmation to its privileges in 1370. This confirmed, not only the University's jurisdictional privileges, but also its international status, involving international recognition of its degrees, and that crucial degree of independence from national government which goes with recognition as an international institution.

Yet, for all the assertions of independence, the University's dependence on the Crown, at least in a unified national state such as England, was too clear to be denied. Professor Southern has remarked that 'no single cause had so much influence on the development of higher studies as the demands of government'.[4] This was not only because of the need for educated people, though that was real enough. It was also because of the natural bargain between Government and learned men: 'you defend me with the pen, and I will defend you with the sword'. The Crown constantly stood in need of written defence, while the privileges of the University, however many times the Pope might confirm them, could not be made effective unless they were enforced by the Crown.

Thus the pattern so familiar to us now, of high assertion of intellectual independence, combined with a total physical dependence, was already established in the first hundred years of University history in this country. A royal writ in 1334 referred to 'the King's Universities' of Oxford and Cambridge. When this is set beside the assertion of the royal charter of 1355, that without wisdom, which was the product of learning, the power of the sword was like a ship caught in a storm without a helm,[5] we have a combination of forces not fundamentally different from that found in the Lord Chancellor's speeches in 1988.

Since the privileges of Universities were so much associated with the Church, reaction against the Church, tended to carry with it an implied threat to the autonomy of the Universities. Marsilius of Padua, in the fourteenth century, complained that 'bishops today . . . subject Colleges of learned men to themselves, withdrawing them from their allegiance to secular rulers, and use them as a slight, but very powerful, means to defend and perpetuate their usurpations against secular rulers'.[6] As Dr Smalley put it,

> his remedy for the evil was not academic freedom, but civil control. Education ought to be a function of lay society, subject to the secular government just as much as any other matter touching the public welfare. Willing commitment to the State should replace corrupt subservience to the church.[7]

The voice of Marsilius has been heard again in the last few years.

During the hundred years or so after the Reformation, when allegiance to the State could realistically be identified with allegiance to the State's religion, and even to the State's wife, academic freedom was perhaps under greater pressure than it has ever been before or since. The University of Oxford, with magnificent reluctance to adapt to a changing world, told Henry VIII that his case for a divorce was invalid, and brought itself into worse disfavour than it has ever been in since. From then on, every change of regime was liable to be accompanied by a purge of Heads of Houses, and an exodus of Doctors of Divinity. Since even civil allegiance to the State was held to be at risk in some of the principal fields of academic study, the State did not feel free to leave them alone. At the same time, the spread of patronage into ever more fields of life made appointments to Headships of Houses, and even to Fellowships, subject to the ebb and flow of court faction.

In practice, things were nothing like as bad as these words might suggest: at any time, people whose views were in disfavour survived, with caution, and sometimes protected their academic freedom by migration into the less controversial medical faculty.[8] Indeed, the increasing apparent danger of theological studies may well have contributed to the growth of the less dangerous scientific subjects of study. Edward Hyde's friend Thomas Triplet, when turned out of the vicarage of Washington (Durham) by the invading Scots in 1640, wished he had stuck to Galen and Hippocrates, and said: 'I am sure I had quack'd safer than I have done now',[9] and he may have spoken for many others. Yet, even if things were by no means desperate, a plea of academic freedom could not be offered to defend theological work in a religion out of favour with the State. Religious pressure on academic freedom continued, with steadily diminishing intensity, until the nineteenth century. In the eighteenth century, the Scottish example, and especially that of Edinburgh, cast doubt on the need for theological tests for University membership. The example of University College, London, though highly controversial at first, was successful in extending a Scottish idea to England. Gladstone's abolition of the theological tests for Oxford and Cambridge brought the era of theological tests in effect, to an end. The century since then has perhaps been a golden age of academic freedom, underpinned by economic growth. The question we face now is whether the slow-down in western economic growth since the oil crisis of 1973, like Henry VIII's divorce, has marked the beginning of another Little Ice Age for academic freedom.

The citadel of academic freedom is of course the principle enshrined in the Academic Freedom amendment: the freedom for academics within the law to question and test received wisdom, and to put forward new ideas and controversial or unpopular opinions without placing themselves in jeopardy. It is the freedom to follow a line of research where it leads, regardless of the consequences, and the corresponding freedom to teach the truth as we see it, with suitable acknowledgment of views which differ from our own. This is as essential to academics as it is to lawyers to be able to say: *fiat iustitia: ruat caelum*. Without the basic principle, the whole system would have no *raison d'être*. The use of having judges depends entirely on the willingness of the public to believe that their judgements represent the law as they see it: were this to be otherwise, contempt of court would become the normal state of affairs. Any judge who listens to private ministerial whispers, saying: 'Of course I understand there's a case against us, but it would be *very inconvenient* if you said so now', risks destroying the whole public acceptance of the legal system. It is for this reason that judges who listened to what seem to have been very oblique and tentative representations from the Crown, and judged for the King against Hampden in

18

the Ship Money case found themselves impeached. In individual terms, this may be thought to have been hard on them, especially since there was a legal case for judging as they did. Yet the mere fact that they had listened to pleas of convenience from the Crown, delivered at second hand through the Chief Justice of the Common Pleas, made it impossible ever to be certain that they had judged for the King because his case had convinced them. For that reason, if for no other, they had to be impeached.

Similarly, an academic who listens to pleas of convenience before publishing his research risks calling in doubt the whole of his determination to find the truth. If academic research is not devoted to finding the truth, it is a form of propaganda, and not necessarily to be preferred to other forms, much cheaper and perhaps more persuasive. Academic research is a laborious, expensive and time-consuming way of investigating problems. It can only be justified on the ground that those who undertake it have been trained to put the attempt to get it right above all other considerations whatsoever. This is not, of course, the same thing as a claim that they *have* got it right: most academics have not, and other academics spend their lives pointing out that they have not. Academic exchange, like parliamentary life, is a process of perpetual debate. Like parliamentary life, it can only be sustained on the ingrained assumption that the participants do not lie. In neither case, of course, is this assumption invariably correct. Yet it is essential, in both fields, that it should be sufficiently often correct to remain the normal working assumption. If it does not, the whole operation will grind noisily to a halt.

The plea of convenience need not always come from the Government. It might come, for example, in research dealing with a possible genetic base for intelligence, from a worried Vice-Chancellor afraid the research might upset the students. It might come, in cases of medical research, from a pharmaceutical firm, afraid the research might show one of its best-selling drugs to have harmful side-effects. In research on the ozone layer, it might come from a major chemical firm, afraid of losses to its export markets. It might come, as in research into homosexuality, from an outraged public opinion, claiming that the research was saying things too shocking to be given a hearing. All such pleas of convenience, *even if their factual base is sound*, are inadmissible in principle. If they are admitted, they risk destroying the base of the whole discipline, which is the pursuit of knowledge for its own sake.

How far the citadel of academic freedom was ever under siege during the debates on the Education Reform Bill was never agreed between the participants. One junior minister was alleged to have said that 'knowledge for its own sake is no longer the prime concern'.[10] If this were Government policy, it should logically have implied the abolition of all Universities, since the services they provided, and the values they taught, were no longer wanted. However, this view was vigorously disowned by the Lord Chancellor on behalf of the Government, and his denial has, so far, been left to stand.[11] Yet the need to run up the flag over the citadel need not imply a belief that a direct attack on the citadel is at present in progress. It is only if the position of the citadel is correctly established that we can consider what outworks are, and what are not, essential to its defence, and therefore what consequential claims follow from the defence of academic freedom.

The ideal itself also constantly needs reasserting against the pressure of public opinion. Mill, who never suffered from what are popularly regarded as liberal illusions, was constantly stressing the depth and the instinctiveness of the emotion of intolerance, even among those who regarded themselves as fully committed to freedom, 'but . . .'. There was force in his reminder that 'orthodox Christians who are tempted to think that those who stoned to death the first martyrs must have been worse men than they themselves are, ought to remember that one of those persecutors was St. Paul'.[12] Modern defenders of freedom, on occasion, are also not immune from lapses. While the Bill was before Parliament, Mr Digby Anderson welcomed the abolition of tenure on the ground that it would make it easier to get rid of 'anti-business ideologues'.[13] Without in any way wishing to defend 'anti-business ideologues', we may still feel that denying them a right to teach in Universities because of their opinions is an example of the same error which would be committed by anyone who would deny them free speech in Parliament because of their opinions. Champions of an 'enterprise culture' are quite entitled to want to change our national culture by means of the normal rules of persuasion, but they have no more right than anti-racists to do so by means of denying a platform to their opponents.

Others, with more authority and more responsibility, may use more subtle methods backed by the carrot and stick. Lord Swann once recounted a case of a questionnaire which required University staff to spell out how their teaching encouraged 'entrepreneurial enthusiasm'. He remarked: 'this, not surprisingly, caused considerable confusion when it fetched up in various divinity faculties'.[14] Ironically, such questionnaires recall those which used to be addressed to faculties of Divinity under Elizabeth I, in order to find out whether they were

20

teaching their pupils a due sense of the evils of popery. In both senses, a revolutionary State was trying to use the Universities to inculcate a new culture. We are still a long way short of the process by which Burghley, Bancroft or Laud used to vet University questions for disputation in order to find out that the 'right' answers were being arrived at, but the area of similarity is too great for comfort. Academic freedom is incompatible with the use of State authority over Universities to bring about a change of culture. This, of course, does not mean that Governments will ever stop wanting to change cultures, or that it will ever be possible to prevent them from using powers of patronage and reward to bring this end about. Nor, indeed, would it necessarily be desirable to do so, since cultures can no more remain static than anything else. The two important points are that there must continue to be some patronage independent of Government, and that Governments engaged in this process must use persuasion and not authority.

It is in this context that there is force in University claims to jurisdictional independence, and value in the intellectual heritage of the Middle Ages. When Government determination to produce a change of culture is this strong, it is the more important that its claims, however sound, should be tested in debate against a contrary opinion. Indeed, it is only by undergoing such a test that the protagonists of the new culture, whatever it may be, will themselves succeed in understanding fully what change they want to bring about.

This test of powerful debate is unlikely to be effectively met without some degree of University autonomy. Academics, like clergy, depend for their daily bread and butter on the financial patronage of the outside world. For that reason, both groups have always needed a high degree of protection against importunate piper-payers, and therefore have felt the need to develop a very strong doctrine of legal and jurisdictional immunity. It is essential that the daily control of appointment and promotion should not be at the mercy of the Government, or indeed of public opinion. It is not coincidental that some of Oxford's first battles over autonomy were fought out on the issue of the licence to teach. For similar reasons, the choice of set books, if any, the control of examinations, and any control over the content and quality of lectures, must not be under outside control. Control of such things in the hands of any outside power will create a temptation it will not be easy to resist. Equally, if decisions about the day-to-day allocation of money are in the hands of, or subject to the influence of, any outside body, an opportunity to threaten academic freedom is thereby created.

This is why, whenever there have been attempts to impose a new intellectual climate on Universities, they have tended to reassert claims to autonomy which descend from the medieval precedents. These are claims to which the Crown and its representatives remain allergic.

In the case of the University of Hull's attempt to dismiss Edgar Page, the University appealed from the decision of the divisional court, denying the court's jurisdiction to review decisions of the Visitor holding jurisdiction under The University's Charter and Statutes, not under common law or statute: 'the courts did not have jurisdiction to review decisions of ecclesiastical and military courts'. Lord Donaldson of Lymington, Master of the Rolls, rejected this argument, on the ground that 'there must be no Alsatia in England where the King's writ does not run'.[15] Thomas Cromwell, and indeed King John, would have understood exactly the point he was making. The medieval principle demanded an extra-territorial Pope as its guarantor, and his disappearance deprived Universities of a very vital protection. How far an extra-territorial European Court may be able to take over the role formerly exercised by the Pope yet remains to be discovered.

Unless or until the European Court takes over a papal role in the protection of Universities, academic freedom exists, if at all, by the sufferance of the Crown in Parliament. It will be protected, if at all, only in so far as the Crown in Parliament regards it as in its own interest to do so. This is a challenge Universities and their spokesmen have no alternative but to attempt to meet. It is perhaps good that they should do so, because there are difficulties in arguing a claim to academic freedom against the national interest. There are some cases, such as those of the professors imprisoned for refusing to give the Hitler salute at the beginning of lectures, where the claim must be argued against the national interest as perceived by the Government. However, in a free country, such cases are not common. The need to argue a claim for academic freedom in the national interest imposes on University champions an intellectual discipline for which they may be none the worse. It will at least force them to attempt, in their own minds, a distinction between academic freedom and their own self-interest.

The need to argue such a distinction was particularly acute during the debates which arose during the passage of the Education Bill on the issue of University tenure. Seen from the Government's end, the notion of the 'job for life' looked rather like a learned version of the National Dock Labour scheme: a cosy privilege of taking public money for doing nothing. It looked like the classic trade-union featherbedding their training and their ideology had taught them to search for under the bed.

They also saw in the notion of tenure a claim to freedom from the discipline of the market, and, holding the assumptions they did, they supposed that freedom from that discipline would lead almost automatically to the reassertion of original sin: it would lead to a proliferation of 'dead wood' which would choke the growth of saplings smothered beneath it. It also saw tenure as denying University authorities a freedom to manage enjoyed by any private-sector management, and a freedom which they saw as a central condition of efficiency. In the words of the Lord Chancellor: 'the difficulty is that if the University or other institution is met by changed economic circumstances it is hoisted by those circumstances if all its staff have tenure'.[16] These were politically powerful arguments, and they derived much of their power from the values of the world outside Universities. There was considerable difficulty in getting the arguments on the two sides to engage, since they drew on different sets of cultural assumptions, and different ideas about the nature of the business to be carried on.

The heart of the case put up in favour of tenure was argued in terms of academic freedom, and its very essence depended on the difference between University research and the normal constraints of work done for an employer. The heart of this case was the need for ability to research without fear. This case did not depend on any assertion that University employers (or the State) were in fact about to start a campaign to dismiss 'anti-business ideologues', or indeed the holders of any other unpopular opinion. This is why the Government, secure in its sense of innocence of any such intention, could not understand why so much fuss was being made. The point is not that academics may not be dismissed for their opinions: it is that they need freedom from fear that they might be so dismissed. Without it, they cannot be counted on to do their work well. A saint, or indeed a particularly rumbustious sinner, might well succeed in doing his best work under the threat of dismissal. Many people, though, are made of less stern stuff. The temptation to trim unpopular conclusions, to cut out the extra sentence which unambiguously spells out the provocative finding, is one to which most academics are not immune. The certain knowledge that they can only be dismissed for misconduct which in effect amounts to breach of contract is a necessary defence against this.

Most academics know, and are reminded by the roll of honour of their profession, that the urge to the witch hunt is a deep-rooted human emotion, and one which is always liable to erupt unexpectedly. The cases of Galileo and William Harvey are examples sufficient to warn us that it might happen to the best of us. That Galileo may have been partly responsible for bringing it on his own head does not refute the point. Some of the very best research may be done by people whose originality takes the form of a sort of divine bloody-mindedness. They preserve their originality by a contempt for others which others are apt to return in kind. Such people, like the historian J. H. Round, often combine their originality with being extremely difficult colleagues, and the temptation to be rid of them can on occasion be extreme. It is because tolerating such people can on occasion be so difficult that the need for an institutional duty to do so can sometimes become so pressing. Yet without such people, some of the greatest advances made in research would never have happened or might have been put off for centuries.

It is also true that some of the best research, as well as the worst, is capable of running into total blocks, in which what appears to be idleness in fact covers a struggle to break through a conceptual barrier of crucial importance to the research. My father has described a period of two years 'during which it seemed likely that the whole of the rest of my life might be consumed in looking at that blank sheet of paper'.[17] The book which resulted was *Principia Mathematica*, and those two years, however much they might appear totally unproductive, were a very valuable investment of academic time. We are now told that the development of the digital computer would have been impossible without the research.[18] If so, the fact illustrates the ironies at the heart of the notion of 'spin-off'. My father's career is also a reminder that the fact that we live in a supposedly free society is not a guarantee against losing an academic job for holding very unpopular opinions on non-academic subjects. In fact he succeeded in doing this, not once, but twice. He lost his job at Trinity College, Cambridge when imprisoned for his opposition to the First World War. To his great pleasure, Trinity gave it back to him nearly a generation later, but not every academic can be expected to return to the profession at the highest level after an absence of 27 years. He also lost a job at what was then the City College of New York, teaching mathematical logic, because of his views on marriage and morals. If this fate can happen twice, to a scholar of this standing, it can happen to lesser men and women also, and the fear of it can inhibit research.

The big threat here does not come from Government: it comes from public opinion. The itch to be intolerant of something is very deep indeed, and the days when divorce could be seen as grounds for losing an Oxford Fellowship are within living memory. The danger is even more acute in a situation where Universities depend on benefactors. To take a hypothetical example, if the risks of thalidomide had been exposed in a University relying on benefactions from Distillers, the risk to the person doing the research would have been very obvious indeed. Those risks are not necessarily less when the offended benefactor is the Government. It is not necessary to have any formal demand for dismissal, against which protests might be made. A hint, delivered quietly, obliquely and in private might suffice if it were possible to dismiss people without alleging grounds. It is because this would almost inevitably inhibit the pursuit of knowledge for its own sake that the abolition of tenure inevitably carries a risk that those funding research may get slightly less than they pay for. It must be admitted that no such scandal has yet arisen, but we are still living in a world whose intellectual climate has been formed by tenure. Its afterglow will be with us for some time yet. If tenure is not restored, the risk that in 50 or 100 years' time academics will be more subservient, and their research therefore less good, must be regarded as real. This cannot be in the interest of those who fund research, any more than it can be in the interest of academics themselves.

This case is valid within its own terms of reference, but it is very hard to make it engage with the economic case argued by the Government. If the argument were left there, the decision would be a matter of priorities, and since it is very hard to make a decision of priority between two such disparate arguments, the dispute would be very difficult to settle. It is necessary, if the arguments are to join, to engage with the Government's economic case.

That case assumes, within its own terms of reference, that anyone dismissed from a job may go to look for another. It is an outlook, in effect, which assumes the existence of a market. Yet a market must imply the existence of a significant total number of transactions. Without that number, the operations of a labour market may be so distorted as to be meaningless. It is often assumed, whether rightly or not, that because industrial management is a general skill, those who are able to manage in one field will be able to manage in another. Someone who has managed a steel works may, if dismissed, apply to manage a telephone company. Wherever this absence of rigidity does not apply, the labour market ceases to work effectively.

These assumptions do not work in an academic context, because of the exceptionally specialized nature of the knowledge involved. A historian who is dismissed cannot simply apply for the next vacancy for a historian. He will not have the necessary knowledge or the necessary skills. Retraining is no answer to this problem, since it could well take him eight to ten years to acquire them. Funding for retraining at this length would cost as much as tenure. A dismissed historian must look for employment on the history of the same country, the same period, and the same type of history. As the bulk of knowledge increases, this tendency inevitably becomes more acute. A specialist in sixteenth-century German women's history will need to wait for the next job in sixteenth-century German women's history, and this may be an unconscionably long time coming. While this trend may legitimately be regretted, and there is much to be said for attempts to slow it down, it will not be put into reverse unless or until it proves possible to destroy existing knowledge.

The other reason why there is no normal market in academic labour is that the British University sector is so small. When this fact is taken together with current financial constraints, we get a situation in which we may go three years without a single job falling vacant in a mainstream field like Tudor and Stuart English history. In this situation, a dismissed academic's chances of re-employment in his own profession may often be so small as to be negligible. If he has invested 30 years of his life in acquiring skill in, for example, Egyptology, he has a skill which is not marketable because no market in the subject exists. This means that the likelihood that those dismissed from jobs in such subjects will be deprived, not only of their jobs, but of their professions, must be regarded as very high indeed. Even more, there must be a considerable risk of a lifetime's unemployment, which will considerably diminish any saving to public funds resulting from the dismissal. It is unwise to enter into so risky an employment without being guaranteed some economic security in return. Otherwise the bargain is too disadvantageous to the academic.

There is perhaps here a parallel to be made to the case of married women who cease to work in order to bring up children. In doing so, they significantly weaken their chances of re-employment afterwards, not only because of age restrictions on appointment, but also because skills in most fields rapidly become outdated. Married women who cease to work in order to bring up children are classified by the Government as having temporarily withdrawn from the labour market. There is a strong case for arguing that those who accept employment in Departments of Egyptology or of Dutch should be regarded as having made a similar withdrawal. In the case of married women, it is recognized in law that this withdrawal necessarily implies an economic right to maintenance, expressed in the form of alimony and of a right of inheritance. It is recognized, and has been as long as civilization has existed, that it is not reasonable to expect women to marry and remain at home with the children unless they acquire some such rights in the process. It is possible that the case for academic tenure can be defended in very much the same terms. If it is argued that some academics can re-enter the labour market with success, it may be replied that so can some married women who have brought up children. In both cases, they will do so, if at all, at a lower level. Without entering into debate about how far this is a risk which we may legitimately expect people to take, we may say that the difficulty of re-entering the labour market at all is great enough to carry an entitlement to some degree of protection.

Without that protection, both academics and married women with children may become reluctant to take the risks inherent in their occupations. They may also become subject to temptation to play safe; academics may choose subjects, not for their intrinsic interest, but for the employment prospects they may carry. In this, they will probably guess wrongly, and they will certainly be engaged in something much less than the pursuit of knowledge for its own sake. As a result, their research will be the poorer, and those who fund them will be getting something less than what they paid for.

It is the central justification of academic freedom that without it, Governments funding Universities will not get what they pay for. As Lord Swann remarked: 'Governments, after all, don't know how to do research, or how to teach.'[19] That is why they pay others to do it for them. If they pay for the educating of graduates, they must be presumed to want to pay for them to be well educated, which means the graduates must be capable of wanting to pursue knowledge for its own sake. It is only if they have this training that they are likely, if they later become civil servants, for example, to have the intellectual discipline necessary to tell the minister that what he wants to do cannot be done. In the short term, the minister may perhaps not want to be told that, but if it is true, it is better for him to find out sooner rather than later. This is why he needs to have civil servants whom he believes capable of not telling him such a thing unless they believe it to be true. If this ideal is not inculcated into graduates, mere technical training will not make their expertise useful. For example, an engineer who will ignore safety regulations in order to win the favour of his superior is not a useful engineer. One who reports that a bridge will stay up when it will not, because his firm are desperate to complete the contract on time, will not add to his firm's reputation or to their profits. It is not only in the so-called 'unworldly subjects' that the pursuit of knowledge for its own sake is a necessary ideal. The desire to cut corners, just like the desire to suppress freedom of speech, is a very deep-rooted human emotion, and a very great deal of conditioning is needed in order to overcome it. This is one of the reasons why it is useful for undergraduates to be faced with academic discipline, and to know they will meet the question: 'What is your source for that?' If their teachers do not practise this discipline, they may preach it till the cows come home, but will not get it across. It is the example, not the precept, which is infectious.

This is one of the many reasons why teaching is only of University quality if it is also done by those who do research. The self-discipline of scholarship does not come easily to most of us, and, like an eye for fast bowling, it can be preserved only by constant practice. It is only in the act of researching that the prejudices to which most of us are subject are harnessed to the discipline of the evidence. Those who are not doing research very rapidly begin to give vent to their prejudices in the course of their teaching and lecturing. As a consequence, their ability to recognize real originality in their pupils is rapidly diminished. Undergraduates, conforming to the example and not to the precept, would then emerge trained to pay lip-service to the latest prejudice.

It is only if research is undertaken as part of the pursuit of knowledge for its own sake that it is likely to be well done. The moment one suggestive quotation is tailored for fear Professor So-and-so may not like it, the quality of the whole undertaking is called in question. Moreover, since research, by definition, involves finding out what nobody else knows, nobody else can be a competent judge of what needs doing. Even a postgraduate supervisor must expect to find that large numbers of questions he poses lead to dead ends, and that the most rewarding ones are ones of which he has never thought. He may legitimately tell the postgraduate that if he has not read a certain body of sources, his results will not be taken seriously, but this is about as far as his authority extends. The best material in any thesis is likely to be either material of which the supervisor has never heard, or material he thought was not worth looking at, because it was unlikely to shed any light on the question. Only the researcher is capable of judging how the research ought to be done.

It follows that the notion of 'accountability' for research money is necessarily a pipe-dream. It is impossible for any outsider to judge what the researcher needs to do. To take an example which is the *reductio ad absurdum* of this point, there are few people who have made a research discovery of greater significance in theory or practice than Archimedes. He was engaged, not, perhaps in 'blue skies' research, but at least in 'blue water' research, but the practical significance of his discovery was immense. Yet his research methods, in the eyes of any accounting committee, would surely leave a great deal to be desired. In recent times, anyone who took research money for sitting in his bath would surely have been a very strong candidate for the late Senator Proxmire's Golden Fleece award. One can almost hear the exclamations: 'Here, have you heard this one? This guy's taking research money for sitting in his bath. What a rip-off!' Research, in its very nature, is a form of gambling, for the researcher does not know what he is going to find out. If the research is a form of gambling, the financing of it must be a form of gambling also. It is no use asking researchers, as the Ministry of Agriculture and the Agricultural Research Council have in fact done, to estimate the benefits of their projected research in terms of discounted cash flow on an annual basis over 20 years.[20] Any researcher who answers this question should not be funded at all. He knows what he is going to find out, and therefore is not engaging in genuine research, but in a form of sophisticated fraud, in which his results will be dressed up to produce a predetermined result. If he is not in fact aiming at a predetermined result, but merely pretending he is in order to get the money, then he is only engaging in a different fraud.

The recognition that research is a form of gambling, and that money given for it cannot be held accountable, is of course extremely hard to take for the bureaucratic mind, and their values are sound too. Yet, if it is in the nature of the case, it must be accepted. Gambling is financed, not by a guaranteed return, but by the occasional outsider who romps home at 10,000 to 1. The case of Archimedes should be a sufficient reminder that such cases do happen, and that it does not require very many of them to make the financing of research a worthwhile activity. Of course, the Treasury, like other gamblers, cannot know which the successful outsider is going to be. It is of the nature of winners at 10,000 to 1 that one has to back 10,000 starters to get one of them. If this is unacceptable to Government, it must simply cease to finance any research at all. We would then have to buy our research knowledge, ready-made, from France, America, Japan or wherever it might be. The result would be that many of our most able young men and women would go there for their education, and a good many of them would not come back again. It would take some effort to argue that this was in the national interest.

Of course such a position imposes a duty of self-restraint on the researcher. He must, if the bargain is to work, impose a good deal of self-scrutiny and self-restraint on his own request for funds. To take an example from my own research experience, I once became convinced that I needed to do some research in the Archives in Bermuda. Such a request might arouse legitimate suspicion in any grant-awarding body, and would make an ideal first chapter for a novel by David Lodge. Moreover, the belief that I needed to do this was based on hunch, not supported by enquiries from the Archivist. This is not conclusive: one of my most important research discoveries was made in a collection the Archivist did his level best to dissuade me from looking at, on the ground that it could not possibly contain anything of use to me. However, it makes a very weak case for obtaining public funds. Although I believed, and still believe, that I was the only competent judge of whether I needed to work in Bermuda, I decided I could not ask any body responsible for awarding public money to take my word for it, and the work is still not completed.

Researchers must also accept that gamblers have a weakness for putting money on proven winners, and those who take money for a project they do not complete will necessarily find that their next project is not easy to finance. An uncompleted project, though, is not the same as one which produces negative findings. The finding that 'there's nothing down this hole' is a significant one, which may save a lot of trouble to future researchers, and may be of considerable theoretical significance. This is something which those who finance research should recognize if they are to get value for money. Otherwise, they will risk getting negative findings dressed up with a spurious positive content which may lead the rest of us astray for some time.

Research is not an area in which 'the customer is always right', which is why the application of the customer–contractor principle to research is fraught with risks. What the customer wants and what is true may be different, and indeed antithetical, but if the customer does not get what is true, he will not get anything which is of any use to him. The point is that the customer is usually unable to judge what is right. The captain of the *Titanic*, who believed his ship was really unsinkable, was an extremely satisfied customer, but he was none the better for it. Conversely, we are told that when Dr William Harvey discovered the circulation of the blood, his patients decided he was a crank, and deserted him in droves. He may not have improved his reputation by describing his fashionable colleagues as 'shitt-breeches'.[21] He was saved from destitution only by the patronage of King Charles I. The principle that 'the customer is always right' can only apply in fields in which the satisfaction of the customer is the ultimate objective. It cannot be the ultimate objective in fields in which the pursuit of knowledge for its own sake is the ultimate objective. Even in dealing with consumers, the principle that 'the customer is always right' must have limits, as, for example, when the customer is thirsty and the water is polluted. In science, if the object is the satisfaction of the customer, we should stop funding science, and fund science fiction, which does the job far better.

The demand for the teaching of creation science in the United States shows that this issue is not in any way dead. To say this, however, must not be to infringe the academic freedom of creation scientists. The view must not be prohibited, and anyone who is prepared, like Edmund Gosse, to work on the task of producing an internally consistent explanation of the evidence which conflicts with it should be free to do so. Creation science cannot be excluded from the 'controversial or unpopular' opinions protected by the Academic Freedom amendment. What is essential is that a creation scientist must submit to the limits of academic discipline and of peer review: he must set out to prove his case according to the rules of evidence, and, even if his own conviction is ultimately of faith, in the academic arena, he must set out to do so according to the rules of reason. It is only if he can show that he has proved his case according to standards of professional competence that he can justly claim to be persecuted for his opinions.

What neither the creation scientist nor his opponents should be entitled to do is to fall back on the weight of law to prohibit opposing views, or even to secure equal time for their own. Such a plea offered to a State Legislature is, as the lawyers used to put it, *coram non judice*: it is before someone who is not a competent judge. Both sides in this issue must base their claims to a hearing in a University on the plea of academic competence, submitted to an academic audience. The judgement of academic competence will, of course, depend in part on the subject in which it is submitted: the test of academic competence in theology will not be identical to the test of academic competence in geology. The use of this test will ensure that the judgement will not be passed merely on the subject: it will be a test of the professional skill of an individual. It must of course be admitted that there are large numbers of academics who will not be easily convinced of the professional competence of someone they regard as on the wrong side of this question. This, perhaps, is not a bad thing, since fundamental convictions should not be changed at the whim of fashion, or because devotion to fair-mindedness ties one hand behind our backs. What is important is that academics asked to sit on a committee to review any such issue should, before they go into the first meeting, sit down and ask themselves whether it is hypothetically possible that they should be persuaded. It is because some may find it difficult to answer 'yes' to this

31

question that the cult of academic freedom as an ideal needs to be kept unremittingly and remorselessly strong.

The case of creationism illustrates the principle that academic research and teaching should not be held accountable to conventional wisdom or to received ideas. It seems to have been one of the deepest convictions of the late Senator Proxmire that academic research which offended common sense was *necessarily* wrong. If he found a title to a piece of research which *sounded* absurd, he seems to have believed that this was sufficient proof that it *was* absurd. This is an issue which needs to be handled with care. Not all academic research is right, and the fact that the research offends common sense may be a good reason for treating it with suspicion. In some fields, at least, the accumulated weight of human experience is evidence of a sort, and is entitled to consideration before it is overridden.

How far this is true may depend on the field in question. Common sense (so-called) is entitled to more hearing in the human and behavioural sciences than it is in more abstract subjects. It is entitled to more consideration in subjects where the evidence can be observed with the naked eye than in those where it cannot. A common sense rejection of the belief that water is composed of H_2O is of no significance at all: the naked eye outside the laboratory is unable to observe and test the evidence on which the conviction is based. The discovery that the earth goes round the sun was widely resisted by those who believed that every morning and evening they had observed otherwise. This observation is, in the literal sense of the phrase, *prima facie* evidence. It is entitled to a hearing, but is not in any way proof against the demonstration that the appearances on which it is based are deceptive. If that demonstration can be made categorical, the argument from common sense may be conclusively defeated.

We are in a different area when judging the academic claims of Freudian psychology. The ascription of disturbed behaviour to childhood traumas, as a rule of explanation, is subject to the weakness that the patient is often unable to remember the evidence, whose existence the professional extrapolates from a subsequent course of behaviour. Methodologically, the procedure is similar to the way the existence of the planets Neptune and Pluto was deduced from the behaviour of other planets, and specifically from the irregularities of their movements. It is a method which is not necessarily unsound, but it does depend on empirical verification, for which the psychologist will find it difficult to supply objective proof. However, it is a valid reply to this objection that human beings do learn from experience, and that the process of learning from experience carries all the risks and difficulties inherent in the logical principle of induction. It is capable of being clear to anyone who has brought up children that the experience from which they learn goes back much farther into their infancy than any memory of the process they may subsequently retain. I have never yet met anyone who remembered learning to talk, yet it is difficult to deny, either that the process is learnt, or that the language in which it is learnt is that which the child has experience of hearing. There should thus be no inherent *logical* difficulty about the presumption that people's adult characters may be influenced by childhood traumas happening too early in their lives to be remembered. Yet it remains a difficulty in the method that whatever type of trauma is invoked as being responsible for subsequent disorder, it seems to be always possible to find other people who have had a similar experience without any of the subsequent consequences. Whatever correlation there may be between childhood trauma and subsequent disorder is not simply causal: there must be some other factor involved. It is thus still open to the advocate of 'common sense' to allege that people's characters are inherently different, and that such difference may affect their reactions to traumatic events. The assertion is not at present verifiable, but neither is the contrary assertion. We are thus left with an area in which academic research and 'common sense' must continue to engage in dialogue. Both academic research and common sense must make considerable efforts to live up to their names if the dialogue is not to be a dialogue of the deaf, but there is at least a situation in which neither opinion has any claim to condemn the other and attempt to put it out of court.

A great deal of recent tension between the Government and the academic community has concerned research in the social sciences, much of which has involved correlation between an undesirable effect and a social condition. Links between poverty and ill-health, for example, have been a fraught area, and so has any attempt to correlate crime with social conditions. Both these lines of research are subject to the same reservation as Freudian psychology, that not everyone subject to the alleged condition suffers the alleged consequence. There is therefore the same necessity to invoke the distinction between a correlation and a cause. There is the same necessity to start a dialogue between research findings and conventional wisdom. High-quality academics must engage in this sort of dialogue: they must accept that if their findings appear absurd, they must make a much greater effort to justify them to a lay audience in terms which that audience can understand. If they argue, for example, that children taken into care because of suspected abuse must be deprived of their toys because the toys may have ritual or symbolic significance, they must expect an initial reaction of incredulity. If they cannot try to understand that reaction from inside, they will not be able to defend their own findings convincingly, or even to understand them completely. In areas where ordinary human experience may constitute valid evidence, academic opinion must engage with it.

Yet all this may be said without authorizing any restriction on academic freedom. As the academic in this sort of field must engage with ordinary experience, so the politician who invokes ordinary experience must engage with the academic research. It is only necessary to make a cursory reconnaissance to see that 'common sense', as perceived in any one age or country, can have no possible claim to infallibility. Anyone familiar, for example, with the placebo effect in medicine can see how common sense can easily degenerate into self-fulfilling prophecy. The man who came to Cardinal Richelieu with a project for inventing a steam engine was imprisoned in a madhouse, on the ground that the submission of such a project was proof of insanity.[22] The people who were convinced that the earthquake of 1580 had happened, either because England had embraced the Reformation, or because it had not done so adequately or sufficiently, were making the same familiar mistake of confusing a correlation with a cause. It is a mistake to which common sense is even more liable than academic research.

It must, then, be absolutely impermissible to silence academic research because it conflicts with received ideas. Indeed, there is perhaps a greater duty to give it serious attention if it conflicts with received ideas. The point is briefly illustrated by reference to two famous geneticists, Lysenko and Mendel. Lysenko's belief in the inheritance of acquired characteristics, because it fitted the presuppositions of Stalin, became the basis of orthodoxy, and of preferment, for a whole country, and caused damage to Soviet science from which recovery has been slow and extremely painful. Conversely, when Mendel published his findings on inheritance in 1866, they were ignored. They were left forgotten in a local journal until they were rediscovered in 1900 – a reminder that even the process of reinventing the wheel is sometimes academically necessary.

No one suspects the present Government of being under any temptation to repeat the Lysenko case. Yet it is worth recording, as a reminder of the dangers posed to originality by the principle of public funding, if it is not combined with a very strong reassertion of the principles of academic freedom and autonomy. No one suspects the present Government of intending to set out on a process of academic censorship. Yet anyone who listens to a group of academics or postgraduates discussing grant applications will rapidly appreciate that they believe (probably rightly) that ideas and methods which are in fashion are a great deal more likely to attract funding than those that are not. Thus, without any direct impropriety, there is a possibility of swings of fashion very much bigger than can be academically warranted. Because imitators usually end up caricaturing what they imitate, such following of swings of fashion will have a built-in multiplier effect, and the point of the absurd will be reached so much the sooner. Since a counter-culture is rarely proof against a fashion, there must be institutional protection against this process if the quality of work done is not to decline very rapidly. This is why those responsible for academic patronage must be plural: power must be diffused, and held at one remove from the Government which is the ultimate source of funds. A University which wishes to have a Department of Peace Studies (or of War Studies) should be able to be confident that its overall funding is unlikely to be reduced as a consequence of its decision. A research council who wish to give a grant to an outstanding young scholar who wishes to investigate Marxist explanations of the withering away of the State in the Soviet Union (or the genetic basis of intelligence) should be able to do so in complete confidence that they will not find themselves purged as a result of a political agitation. The pluralism and the academic freedom in this situation are interdependent, and whenever academics face a Government which is suspected of wishing to change a culture, such points are legitimately and relevantly reasserted.

Here we have one of the roots of the value of academic freedom to a free society. The political pluralism essential to a democratic society must rest on a foundation of cultural pluralism. Free elections must to an extent rest on a plural structure of political parties, and if these do not rest on differences of ideas, they will be differentiated only by opportunism. Anyone who reads the Sunday newspapers must be aware how far society works on a limited intellectual stock-in-trade of ideas, clichés, stories, heroes and villains. These provide an interpretative framework for new and significant events, and a series of Homeric stock epithets in which a new story can be told. A society without some variety in this intellectual stock-in-trade will be without the means of accurately observing what is happening to it. The point was amusingly illustrated on 19 August 1991, when Boris Yeltsin climbed on a tank outside the

Russian Parliament to declare his opposition to the coup, and a woman watching him murmured in admiration: 'Just like Lenin!'[23]

This argument for pluralism in our stock of clichés is the lowest common denominator of the argument for pluralism, but in a democracy, not necessarily therefore the least important. On a higher level, a Government which is to be subjected to the sort of critical scrutiny democracy demands must not enjoy a monopoly on national culture, or else no one will have the terms of reference needed for any far-reaching criticism. There must be, in any effectively free country, codes of values and systems of belief deeply antithetical to those held by the Government of the day. Without such a conflict to inform parliamentary debate, Governments will not be subjected to the sort of intellectual challenge needed to bring them to understand their own beliefs in any critical way. If this is to be so, there must be independent sources of ideas. It is in this area that the freedom of political parties, churches and Universities rests on a common justification.

This case was made long ago by John Stuart Mill. He wrote:

> Every function superadded to those already exercised by the government, causes its influence over hopes and fears to be more widely diffused, and converts, more and more, the active and ambitious part of the public into hangers-on of the government, or of some party which aims at becoming the government. If the roads, the railways, the banks, the insurance offices, the great joint-stock companies, the universities and the public charities, were all of them branches of the government; if, in addition, the municipal corporations and local boards, with all that now de-volves on them, became departments of the central administration; if the employés of all these different enterprises were appointed and paid by the government, and looked to the government for every rise in life; not all the freedom of the press and popular constitutions of the legislature would make this or any other country free otherwise than in name.[24]

This is why, since a combination of greater economic equality and more capital-intensive systems have made it essential to fund a number of these bodies from public funds, it has been recognized as essential to have a system of accountability which keeps direct Government intervention at arm's length. This was the point of the old University system of block grants, abolished in the 1988 Act, under which money was granted for teaching and research; and it had to be shown that it was used for those purposes, but central accountability went no further down the line.

Mill's main concern, like that of Universities, was with freedom of thought, yet he recognized in this passage the vital link between freedom of thought and institutional autonomy. Loyalty to a Government is a very strong force. So too is the desire to conciliate the holders of power: most people hold, in the words of A. H. Clough:

Honour thy parents: that is all
From whom advantage may befall.

(‘The Latest Decalogue’)

This should be set beside my father's remark that ‘Most children desire to please. If they did not, all discipline would be impossible.’ It is because these instincts are carried over into adult life, where they are constantly reinforced by arguments of economic and professional prudence, that the potential hold of a Government over its subjects is so strong, and resisting it in isolation is so difficult.

This is where it is essential to a politically plural society that most of us should have other centres of loyalty as well as the Government. Historically, much of the most effective challenge to Governments and their values has come from corporations and associations. The pattern was set for western society by the autonomy of the Church. Magna Carta Clause 1 ‘*Quod ecclesia Anglicana libera sit*’, that the English Church should be free, has set an ideal on to which other corporate bodies can graft themselves, the Universities among their number. People usually associate in one of two ways, either by occupation or by locality, and this fact is mirrored in the associations and groupings which have been able to challenge Government. It is appropriate that in this passage, Mill put together Universities and Local Government. The last English ruler who challenged both at once, was James II, and he did not survive the experience for very long. The point is still topical. In the night of 19–20 August 1991, Soviet armour was attacking the barricades around the Russian Parliament building. It seemed likely at the time, as we now know to be the case, that this was an exploratory attack, designed to test the morale and determination of the defenders and see whether they would stand their ground. It was at this point, when the leaders of the coup must have been hoping that the defenders would begin to melt away, and when it had just been learnt that three people had been killed defending one of the outer barricades, that the BBC cameras picked up a large crowd of young people vigorously making their way towards the point of danger. There were undergraduates from Moscow University, rallying to the defence of their parliament building. Universities are as essential a part of resistance to despotism in 1991 as they were in 1688.

Anyone making claims of this magnitude risks sounding holier than thou. This is why, in all centuries, people have thought to defeat the claims of the Universities, and of the Church before them, by showing that many of their adherents had feet of clay. Yet in fact it is precisely because Universities, and the Church, are made up of people no better than the rest of us that they need the constant invocation of such high ideals as a necessary professional discipline. Both professions suffer from a total economic dependence on the outside world. That economic dependence accentuates the effect of the ordinary hopes and fears to which all people are subject, and has given both professions their full share of Vicars of Bray.

Equally, academics are as subject as the rest of us to the desire not to appear fools. The imitative quality now known as peer-group pressure, is the quality which makes groups of people so vulnerable to pressure to dress, talk or think alike, and it is one which, in academic life, tends to prop up established orthodoxies. Anyone who sends a piece of research to press which challenges one of these orthodoxies head-on knows that the price of failure will be a very considerable load of ridicule, if not worse. This knowledge, like other fears, generates a very large amount of touching wood. The wood which is touched in this situation is usually the basic code of academic freedom, the belief in the pursuit of knowledge for its own sake. This makes those who contemplate the head-on challenge to orthodoxy believe that they are doing what their professional discipline demands. Also, it makes them believe that rewards will await success. Thus the code of academic freedom is often necessary to the production of truly original work, as well as to its protection when published.

Because academics are no better than other people, they have their full share of human intolerance. The urge to forbid what we dislike to the point of hatred is very deep, and probably instinctive, and the passions generated by academic controversy bear witness to the fact. This is not only *odium theologicum*, strong though that emotion is. Very few academics have the intellectual detachment to admit that major portions of their own work have been refuted, and their desire to protect what they come to regard as their own turf is as strong as that of any Whitehall bureaucrat. It is only because these battles are fought out before a professional jury which is itself schooled in the principles of academic freedom that they can be kept under control. Stories are sometimes told of senior scholars trying to prevent publication of work by junior scholars which challenges their own. What is vital is that we live in an intellectual climate in which such stories put the mark of Cain upon the senior scholar of whom they are told: they discredit him with his professional peers, and hoist a signal that refuting him is fair game. Were this not so, academic intolerance would be a very much more dangerous force than it is. Because the pen, like the sword, can kill, it too needs its code of chivalry.

These, then, are the ideals into which Governments are asked to put their money. They will only do so if they can see that some advantage comes to them from doing so. What might be their motives? On the lowest level, in a democratic society, they may choose to do so because a strong demand exists. This is a demand which exists in ministers' constituencies, and may be reinforced by its reiteration by their sons and daughters. In a democratic society, it is not improper that such a demand should be listened to. It gains force from the fact that, since 1945, the educational system has taken over from heredity many of the functions of a social selector: it is engaged in picking out the people who will hold the privileged posts in the next generation. In other words, it has taken over many of the functions which used to be discharged by the College of Heralds who conferred gentility in England by recognizing the right to use a coat of arms. When two out of four people who have held the office of Prime Minister since 1974 are not University graduates, this theme should not be exaggerated. If we are not to have a mandarin caste system, it is equally vital that it should never become uniform. There should always be a way through for those who fell off the escalator at 15, at 17 or at 21. If this is not so, there will be a vital and unnecessary waste of talent.

Yet, when this is said and allowed for, in any society, there must be some method of selection for the people who will be in the running for prominent positions in the next generation. Heredity does not now command general confidence as a system of selection. Patronage is a possible alternative, yet 1991 does not seem a particularly likely date for Britain to go over to a system of *nomenklatura*. In fact, in a society whose standards of fairness are not based on birth or position or contacts, it is hard to see an alternative to using the educational system for this process of selection. So long as it is so used, it is of considerable importance to the country's future that the minds which emerge from it should be as well trained as possible. Other things being equal, it is better that our civil servants, judges, journalists, industrial managers and so forth should be people with ability and a competent general intellectual training than without them. If that objective is dependent on academic freedom, then Governments have a considerable incentive to respect academic freedom.

It may be suggested, in passing, that this view of the uses of Universities to society may provide a brake on their expansion. Unless we are to produce a marked extension of the type of jobs seen as needing to be filled by graduates, and move towards the alleged New York situation of taxi drivers with doctorates, some brake may be placed on expansion by the limited number of jobs graduates are likely to regard as fitting for them. A large production of graduates unable to find jobs which fit what they see as their dignity are likely to produce a discontented, if not alienated, force which may cause some difficulty.

The arguments which may be put to Governments to show why they might respect academic freedom, then, do not depend on any direct benefit to the economy as a result of academic research. The desire to have a good selector for those holding prominent posts in the next generation may be sufficient. If that depends on the union of teaching and research, that fact alone might be a sufficient justification of research. The techniques inculcated through it, like play among children, may be a vital preparation for tasks to be undertaken in adult life.

Yet, though the justification of research need not depend on its direct economic benefits to society, these can be shown to be very considerable. If radar and penicillin were the only beneficial results of research since 1940, it would not be impossible to argue that they alone have produced benefits sufficient to justify the money spent by Governments on research. Without radar, we would not have won the Second World War. It is not necessary to attempt to quantify what we would have lost by losing the war to argue that something which changed the result of the war was of direct benefit to the country. This benefit neither can nor should be expressed in terms of gross national product. Yet anyone who has flown to do business abroad must acknowledge the contribution of radar to the gross national product. Any costing of the benefit of penicillin to the gross national product must be hypothetical, since it must rest on a calculation of who would have died if it had not been available.

If it were necessary to rely on these arguments alone, it might be enough. Yet they are not alone. A survey conducted by the Japanese Ministry of International Trade, reported in February 1985, investigated the national origins of inventions of commercial significance since 1945. The resulting figures were Britain 55 per cent, US 22 per cent, Japan 5 per cent.[25] These figures seem to show that whatever else is responsible for Britain's poor economic performance since the war, it is not our Universities. Even though economic progress is a by-product of University research, rather than its central justification, it is a by-product which, in strictly commercial terms, might well justify the Government money which has been spent on research. In investing in the maintenance of academic freedom, Governments are not being asked to give something for nothing.

2

THE LIMITS OF ACADEMIC FREEDOM

The decision on how much to spend on higher education is essentially a 'political' decision.

> (Robert Jackson, MP, *Times Literary Supplement*,
> 30 December 1988)

The principle that rights carry duties is not incapable of exception: the right to vote, for example, neither does nor should carry with it a duty to exercise the right. Yet, as a general principle, it is a good one. Certainly, those invoking academic freedom must be willing to admit, both that the principle imposes duties on academics directly, and that it carries a duty to respect the reciprocal rights of others, including both our pupils and the Government which is being asked to foot the bill.

There are certain obligations which must rest upon academics as a consequence of the ideal of academic freedom itself. For some breaches of these ideals, they are answerable to the authorities of their institutions, and for some they can be held answerable only at the bar of academic opinion. There must, though, be some others for which they cannot claim jurisdictional autonomy, but must submit to the discipline of the common law. The Academic Freedom amendment enshrined a right to 'freedom within the law', and the limitation is significant.

Freedom to pursue knowledge for its own sake must carry a concomitant duty of truthfulness. In reading any academic work, we normally take a vast amount on trust. We do not normally have access to a scientist's notebook with his rough workings. In believing that his findings are accurately reported, we depend on trust, fortified by the ability of any other scientist to repeat the experiment and see whether it produces the same result. In believing that a historian's findings are accurately reported, we will be taking his word for the contents of documents cited from what may be 20 or 30 manuscript archives, some of them many thousand miles away. Normally, in accepting this evidence, we will be taking his word for it, fortified by the ability of any other scholar visiting the archive to look up the document quoted, and see whether the words alleged are accurately quoted. Any serious check will then go on to see what else is in the document which has been left out. Except in the main printed sources, such checks do not happen as often as perhaps they should, and erroneous work may sometimes stand for many years before anyone discovers its flaws. Under these circumstances, the ability to trust one's fellow scholars is of very considerable importance. Though truth in history is a very shadowy commodity indeed, error is often plain enough: if, for example, the word 'not' is left out in a transcription, there is no room for argument about whether this is an error.

It is doubtful whether there is any historian alive who has not committed error, though the only error to which the late K. B. MacFarlane ever admitted was the very venial error of confusing two Suffolk villages with the same name. No historian should be penalized for simple, honest error. What can be required of him is that he should not make a habit of it. He may find, and certainly should find, that if he does make a habit of it, his footnotes are checked more frequently, and his applications for grants are more critically scrutinized.

What is a great deal more serious, and calls the basis of academic freedom in question, is wilful error perpetrated deliberately for the sake of advancing a career or a cause (it tells us something significant about academics that advancing a cause is probably the more common motive of the two). It is, unfortunately, extremely difficult ever to be certain that any colleague has *deliberately* committed error. It is only in extreme cases, like falsification of results of experiments or citation of imaginary documents, that a charge of deliberate error can be proved. When such charges can be proved, however, they undermine the grounds on which the whole profession is supported, and should be regarded as grounds for dismissal, even from a tenured post. Where deliberate error is strongly suspected, but cannot be proved, it is right that the suspect should find the marks of professional honour drying up. He should find that he is not asked to give papers at conferences, to review books, to referee papers for learned journals, to write letters for colleagues' promotion, or to accept all the other innumerable marks of trust the profession showers upon its successful sons and daughters.

Yet, because the charge of falsifying references or results is so damaging, those who make it and cannot sustain it do and should come within the realms of the common law. Academic freedom confers no exemption from the laws of libel and slander. A profession which justifies itself by its duty to search for truth cannot claim any legal immunity from action for wilful breaches of that duty. To say a colleague has falsified his references when he has not is liable to bring him into hatred, ridicule and contempt, and so is legally actionable. In fact, academics usually choose not to bring actions for such things, because it is the judgement of their peers that they really want to win, and calling in outside assistance, like calling in the teacher in the playground, does not always win the approval of their peers. Yet the right is and must be there. If we are to dissuade our colleagues from exercising it, the weight of academic disapproval against those who make such charges and cannot sustain them must be palpable. In extreme cases, it would be defensible to regard it as ground for dismissal from a tenured post.

Similarly, there can be no mercy for a proven charge of plagiarism. Again, the offence is against the basis of academic freedom, and it is only if it is severely dealt with that the profession as a whole can claim that it is doing what it is supposed to do. Anyone who claims to have done a piece of research is claiming trust, and it is an abuse of that trust, as well as an injury to a third party, if he simply lifts the findings from someone else. Again, the offence should be grounds for dismissal. Again, the common law remains available in the background if sufficient remedy is not found within the academic community, and now that the courts more clearly recognize the concept of intellectual property, remedy should be available. If the offence is to be stamped out, the task must be begun early. Undergraduates who copy passages from their set books and pass them off as their own sometimes are alarmingly unaware that they have done anything wrong: indeed, I have been faced, when teaching, with plagiarism taken *verbatim* from my own work, which cannot have been expected to evade detection. On the first offence, it should be explained clearly what is wrong, and the second offence should be given a failure mark. It is not academic work, but theft.

Academic freedom within the law must also entail a recognition of the right to free speech. In addition to the common-law protection provided by the offence of breach of the peace, free speech now enjoys a specific statutory protection. There is room for debate about where and on whom the duty of ensuring free speech should be imposed, since no one should be saddled with a duty they are not legally able to discharge, and Vice-Chancellors do not normally enjoy powers of arrest. Yet, though there may be room for discussion about how the principle should be enforced, there should be none at all about the principle itself. A right to assert 'controversial or unpopular opinions' must necessarily carry a duty to respect that same right in others. This right is not merely essential to the political process in a democracy: it is also of the essence of the academic process itself. A freedom to engage in the pursuit of knowledge for its own sake must carry a corresponding duty to recognize that same right in others. It must, then, carry an obligation to answer arguments which fill us with moral outrage (and there will always be such arguments), not by enforcing silence, but by debate and the use of evidence. The silencing of an opponent sounds alarmingly like an admission that we cannot answer him. Any academic who sells this particular pass has forfeited any right to complain if the Government intervenes in University life and does the same thing itself. If free speech may be silenced, the contest will be won, not by the better argument, but by the greater power. This is not an academic contest at all.

The limitation on free speech, like the limitation on academic freedom, is that it must be within the law. An impassioned appeal to storm the Dean's office is an incitement to riot, and no amount of respect for free speech makes it permissible. A speech alleging that Professor X falsifies examination results for money must expect to be tested by the law of libel, and damages may be severe if the claim cannot be sustained. A claim that our existing political system is rotten to the core and should be swept away is within the legitimate limits of free speech, and should be answered by argument and not by force. An argument that our existing political system is rotten to the core, and therefore that the crowd should storm Downing Street, on the other hand, is an incitement to riot. By urging the audience to go beyond free speech, it forfeits the protection for free speech. The basic principle is as Mill stated it:

> an opinion that corn-dealers are starvers of the poor, or that private property is robbery, ought to be unmolested when simply circulated through the press, but may justly incur punishment when delivered orally to an excited mob assembled before the house of a corn-dealer.[1]

The taking of money for teaching and research also imposes a duty to engage in those activities. This is, of course, in the first instance a contractual duty to the employer, who has a remedy if it is not discharged. If the employer is funded by the State, it may also be seen as a duty to the State. It is, of course, notoriously difficult to prove how far academics discharge their contractual duty to engage in research, especially in those subjects, such as history, where research is still properly a cottage industry. Publication is a proper yardstick, but it is not the only one. The amount of research which goes into one article is capable of extreme variation. There is a strong case for the view that too much is now being published, and that pressure to publish results only in filling more journals with work which is not always of the very highest significance. It is also true that many of us know colleagues who, to our certain knowledge, engaged in research, but have an almost negligible publication output to show for it. We may know they are doing research from conversation, in which they regularly have archival information which others do not have, from papers they give in academic gatherings, and indeed from regularly meeting them in the British Library or the Public Record Office. To require them to publish, when the bulk of publication is growing so extremely, may seem harsh, especially since many of them are very knowledgeable and shrewd scholars, whose judgement is widely accepted. It should also be borne in mind that research, like other creative activity, may be cyclical: a burst of extreme activity in research may be followed by a fallow period in which the scholar does almost nothing in the research field. This must remain legitimate, since there would be very much less good work done without it. Yet if persistent and long-term failure to do research can be shown, that must be recognized as an abuse of academic freedom. No one has the right to take money for things they do not do. Whether this principle applies in any particular case is something which only academics in the same field can judge.

Failure to discharge teaching duties is very much easier to prove, and must carry similar strictures. This need not mean we should carry things to the length of the proverbial Oxford College tutor, who was once telephoned in the middle of a tutorial, and replied: 'I'm sorry, dear: I can't do anything now: I'm teaching.' An agitated noise emerged from the telephone, to which he replied calmly: 'Have you sent for the fire brigade, dear?' Such devotion to duty is not legitimately required, but performance of duty is, and the principle of academic freedom will not excuse failure to discharge the duty.

The academic community must also concede that the State, as well as the Universities, has rights. By far the most important of these is that it is the State's task to determine the amount of money to be spent on Universities. So far as I know, no academic has ever cast doubt on this principle, but since it is a central point in the task of striking a balance between Universities and the State, it needs reiterating. It is true, in the first place, for constitutional reasons. The principle of taxation by consent must underpin any democratic government, and in this country, that consent is properly expressed in Parliament, where the

Government of the day enjoys a majority. This means, in practice, that ministers decide how much money, if any, should be devoted to each and every object of public expenditure. If, as very often happens, people wish to challenge the grand total of sums committed to public expenditure, this is something which must be done in the first instance through Parliament, and ultimately through the ballot box.

This principle underlies each and every object of public expenditure. If, for example, the Government were to decide to spend no public money on the Police, or on the imprisonment of criminals, and therefore to repeal all laws at present carrying the penalty of imprisonment, there would, no doubt, be a substantial public outcry to the effect that this decision was unwise and unwelcome. However, under the doctrines of parliamentary sovereignty and ministerial responsibility, there is no way it could be argued that a Government had no *right* to do it: remedial action would have to wait until the next election, unless members of the Government's majority, at the risk of losing their own seats, were to force a Government defeat. This, of course, is something members of the governing majority hardly ever do. In the British political system, any argument that a Government has no right to do anything is a cock which will not fight, save in the single case of rights guaranteed by international treaty obligation.

This means that neither the University system as a whole nor individual Universities in particular can claim any right to exist at all. The precedent of the monasteries must surely establish this. They, like the Universities, were corporations owning their own property. This did not make an Act of Parliament dissolving them and expropriating their property *ultra vires*. The Universities are very much less entrenched in our national life than the monasteries were in 1536, and an act dissolving one is as much within parliamentary competence as an act dissolving the other. If Parliament should decide that Universities have outlived their usefulness, and the country does not need any more of them, there is no constitutional obstacle to its putting its will into effect.

Since the greater includes the less, there is no constitutional obstacle to a Government decision, backed by an ever-obedient majority, to close any single University. The only exceptions are the Universities of Edinburgh, Glasgow, St Andrews and Aberdeen, whose existence has been guaranteed 'for ever' by the Act of Union between England and Scotland, in 1707.[2] The Act of Union was, in constitutional form, an international treaty, and therefore such a guarantee could, in theory, be binding on Parliament. However, it was the central weakness of the Act of Union that it did not leave behind it any Scottish guaranteeing party:

the successor State to the Scottish Parliament is the Union Parliament at Westminster. As that Parliament knows well, no Parliament can bind its successors. A parliamentary guarantee 'for ever', then, could only mean a parliamentary guarantee until Parliament chooses to change its mind. Thus the only way in which Edinburgh, Glasgow, St Andrews and Aberdeen are any better off than other Universities is that their closure requires legislation. While this would no doubt be inconvenient to the Government, clogging up parliamentary time with protests from the opposite parties, and perhaps with Scottish Nationalist demands for the repeal of the Act of Union, it would be no worse than inconvenient. The Government majority would doubtless soldier through.

All this is a consequence of the fact that our constitution recognizes no rights save those conferred by Parliament. No University has a natural right to exist, and there is no right to a University sector of any specified size. Were the Government to decide, for example, that they wanted no Universities in the country save Oxford and Cambridge, there would be nothing to stop them having their own way. Since the greater includes the less, it must follow that there is no obligation on the Government to provide any particular level of funding for Universities. This principle must also follow from the fact that it is the Government's duty, not only to fix the total level of public spending, but to weigh competing claims against each other.

The maximum which *could* be spent on Universities is small. In 1989, the total amount of private spending in the country was £315 billion, and the percentage of this which even the most dedicated public service Government can afford to devote to public-spending increases must be limited: something must be left to sustain an economy, and to give people something to live on. Any opposition party, listing things whose proponents argue, for compelling reasons, that they *must* be done, would have no difficulty in running up a list of spending commitments amounting to some £100 billion. Since the maximum increase which could be contemplated might be a fifth of that, any claims for University spending will be bidding against claims to increase the level of Social Security benefits on the ground that they have fallen below subsistence level, or to resurrect London Regional Transport to a point where it can get Londoners to work. Since it is every public service, and not merely Universities, which are funded well below the minimum level at which they can function efficiently, the task of adjudicating between competing claims will be one of exceptional difficulty. It is the resolving of this sort of contest which is the specialist skill of politicians, and in common sense, as well as in constitutional theory, it is hard to argue a case that the

47

task should fall on anyone else. This means that the Universities have a dependence on Government from which there is no safe escape, and which necessarily constrains their bargaining power. As one cross-bench peer put it, 'it's no use getting tough with your bank manager'.

With the Government's right to determine the total amount spent comes its right to accounting to determine that the money has been used for the purposes for which it was granted. As the Lord Chancellor said, while the Education Bill was going through Parliament, the House of Commons 'which votes the funds, must be able to be satisfied that they are used for the purposes intended, and in accordance with financial proprieties. That must be right.'[3] This is not a matter of dispute between the Government and the academic community. When the Lord Chancellor moved an amendment to allow the Universities' accounts to be open to the Comptroller and Auditor General, none of the numerous academic peers who took part in the resulting debate expressed any reservations about the general principle involved.[4] The reservations expressed were entirely about how the principle could usefully be applied, not about its propriety or even its necessity.

To see the necessity for this principle, it is only necessary to remember some of the cases of abuse of public money which have come to light in other fields of Government spending, for example Local Government. Taking money for services not rendered is, very properly, a crime. The existence of any large sums of public money without adequate accounting is a standing temptation to that crime, and it was not only Oscar Wilde who could resist anything except temptation. Since academics are no better than other people, they are no more immune from temptation than other people. The fact that, on the whole, the academic community has been remarkably free of corruption cannot be presumed to be going to continue. Restraints which apply to everyone else must apply to academics too. They have no claim to be above the law.

The question is not whether there should be accountability: it is what form accountability should take. There is no dispute about letting the Comptroller and Auditor General see the Universities' accounts. There is no question that money taken for teaching and research must be spent on teaching and research, subject only to reasonable allowance for window-cleaning, heating and such activities as are incident to running any institution with premises. The question, in discussing accountability in any public-service body, is what ought to be accounted for at what level. Accounts may be audited centrally, at Research Council or Funding Council level, at University level, or at departmental level.

Decisions may be taken about allocation of money at any of these levels. The question of who audits what and when then becomes a question of the degree of decentralization permitted within a publicly funded enterprise. This is a question with application far wider than the University sphere. The case for decentralization of decision-making may be particularly strong in Universities, because such a high proportion of decisions taken must necessarily depend on particular knowledge and specialist expertise. This is true even within a University, which is why the position of Head of Department is one in which it is often possible to make more difference to what happens than that of College Principal. A very high proportion of decisions are what the army would call operational, and therefore have to be taken by the senior person actually in the field. There is sense, then, in arguing that decisions ought to be taken on the level where the expertise necessary to take them is most likely to be present. There is corresponding sense in arguing that accounts ought to be audited on the level on which decisions are actually taken. It is only in that way that those who actually take the decisions can be appropriately held accountable for the decisions they take.

This, like any other case for administrative decentralization, of course creates some difficulties in Whitehall, and especially in the Treasury. Just as academics are often single-minded in their pursuit of freedom to research, so the Treasury is often single-minded in its pursuit of accountability for public money. Others besides Universities have complained of Civil Service approaches to accountability. Mr D. J. Dickinson, of the London East Training and Enterprise Council, complained that 'historically they have always tried to follow the money right down the chain as far as it can go with their own control systems'. This was not a plea for Training and Enterprise Councils (TECs) to be unaccountable: it was a plea for them to be held accountable at a lower level, and for the process of accountability not to be confused with policy directions about the use of the funds. The Lord Chancellor's phrase, that the money ought to be used for the purpose intended, is capable of a great variety of meanings, depending on how tightly the purpose intended is defined. Much of Mr Dickinson's argument was that the purpose was being too tightly defined. He said:

> The question of responsibility without power, or power without responsibility, is an issue which leads to confusion. The Army describes it very simply as order plus counter-order leads to disorder. Where you have two people both believing they are controlling the same thing, you may find that neither of them control that thing. So what I am arguing the case for is that TECs

should have total responsibility for their money, they should be accountable for it, they should be thoroughly audited, and they should not be interfered with, they should not be given instructions by a centralist system telling them what to do against their better judgement, where people can have power without taking responsibility.

Mr Dickinson was not arguing against accountability: he explained that 'what I am saying is that systems should be put in place that are to the highest standard of the private sector managing of money, and this means everything must be scrupulously audited'.[5] He was making the same point as Sir Peter Swinnerton-Dyer, arguing that businessmen on the Universities Funding Council would be 'particularly unamused' by the accounting practices required of them by the Treasury.[6] They were arguing, from the point of view of private industry, that accountability was being used as a cloak for the pursuit of power. *Mutatis mutandis*, it is the same argument which was put up on behalf of the Universities by Lord Swann and others. The road to the planned economy is paved with good intentions.

The case for decentralization in the management of public services is that put on behalf of the Universities by Lord Dainton, speaking as a former Chairman of the University Grants Committee: 'decisions taken at the centre, remote from the laboratory bench, the lecture theatre or from the tutorial groups were generally ill-informed'.[7] It has many points in common with the free-market case that decisions taken by planning at the centre are generally less efficient and less responsive to circumstances. Similarly, a free market in ideas depends on the decentralization of decision-taking. The more decentralized decisions are, the quicker and the more spontaneously they can be taken. In scientific research in particular, where it may matter so much to the country that one scholar seizes the opportunity before another, this can be of the highest importance. Otherwise, academic research would risk going the way of Soviet agriculture. This means that accountability cannot be used to interfere with the freedom to make decisions at a local level. The need to ensure that those decisions are not made improperly, which auditors can perfectly well do, is not the same thing as an attempt to ensure that they are made well, which an auditor is not competent to do.

The word 'accountable', of course, has more than one meaning. There is the strict and narrow auditor's sense, in which accountability cannot be abandoned. There is also the sense regularly used at Westminster, in which the minister is accountable to Parliament for the discharge of his duties. This sense is very much wider, and involves far more in the way of value judgements about how the system is operated. The minister is accountable to Parliament, not merely for whether his job is done honestly, but for whether it is done well. The two senses of accountability should not be confused, since they raise very different issues. The problem with the wider sense of accountability, in all public services, is to whom they should be held accountable. There is the further difficulty that legal accountability, holding those in charge answerable if they make a mess of it, often does not rest in the same place as practical accountability, the ability to make a crushing response to the provision of poor-quality services. In a private firm, for example, the directors are legally accountable to the shareholders, but practically accountable to the customers. It is not the shareholders who are always right. Any debate on accountability in the public services should take account of both senses. In dealing with the wider sense, we should perhaps consider, not only how far public services can be held accountable, but how far they should be held accountable if they are not to be brought to a standstill.

The problem of accountability in the wider sense is probably most severe in those public services, like water or electricity generation, which are natural monopolies. Here, the problem of potential abuse of power is much more severe in that there is a captive market to exploit. No one can afford not to use water, however disastrous the standards of its provision, and an unregulated monopoly of water would be a licence to print money. In these fields, we do not have an obvious alternative to the Roman consular model of management set opposite regulation, in a perpetual struggle to find out which is the poacher and which is the gamekeeper.

Universities are not in this position at all. They are not a natural monopoly. There is no restriction on any scholar, or on any potential undergraduate, restraining him or her from going to University in another country. If our standards of languages were higher, the ERASMUS scheme for student exchange within the European Community would contribute even more to this. Moreover, there is a competition between British Universities, and it does not need to be economic to be effective. It is part of the standing of a University, and therefore of potential value to it, if it fills up most of its undergraduate places without needing to have recourse to the clearing house. There is here a form of practical accountability. Those who find, as people teaching deconstruction in some English departments in the USA have done, that their teaching promotes a flight of undergraduates, will find that the stature, and therefore the funding of their department is diminished. The professor who is said to have left an English civic University because he was not allowed to work in his room after 5.30 p.m. probably delivered a considerable blow to the standing of that University. The professor who is said to have recently left an English University because he was required to be in his room five days a week, and therefore was effectively forbidden to do research, has certainly lowered the standing of that University in the eyes of his fellow scholars, and may in due course, when the grapevine has done its work, do so in the eyes of potential entrance applicants. This practical accountability exists in many more forms than can be listed here, and its effects constitute a reminder that in traditional English usage, the words 'reputation' and 'credit' used to be synonymous.

This practical accountability, necessary and important though it is, is not in the last resort a substitute for legal accountability. Legal account-ability is something for which the existing models, including the accountability of directors to their shareholders, leave something to be desired. The connection between bad performance and being held accountable, is not quite, like the proverbial resemblance to any living person, purely coincidental, but it approaches it. There is the further difficulty in the accountability of Universities, that Whitehall is simply incompetent to discharge the task. Whitehall cannot tell whether a study of place-names in Herefordshire from the seventh to the tenth centuries is an antiquarian exercise of technical competence but of little significance, or an illuminating study of the differentiation of the English from the Welsh. It does not even know whom to ask about such questions if it wants an expert opinion. This is why, from the first Chancellors of Oxford down to the University Grants Committee, accountability has been handled through an intermediary, involving people whose academic qualifications did make them competent to do the job. There was a very great deal that could be done about an incompetent department without interfering with a University's legal autonomy, and without using any weapon so blunt as a threat to cut off funds. This, however, depended in its turn on the autonomy of the University Grants Committee, and its ability to follow academic stan-dards without too much interference from Whitehall. The disappearance of the built-in academic majority on the old University Grants Committee has made the new Universities Funding Council open to the question whether it is as competent to do its job as its predecessor was. This question in turn prompts pressure for more mechanisms of accountability.

It should be accepted that ministerial responsibility, like Treasury accountability, cannot be taken too far down the line. Whatever the minister is responsible for, in these things he will be tempted, and sometimes pressed, to intervene. Indeed, if he may suffer censure for a particular decision, he must, in self-preservation, want to have a finger in that decision. This means that the system of ministerial responsibility constantly leads the minister into temptation to intervene in the sort of detailed issue which, in a well-run system, he should leave to be settled at a lower level. There is nothing new about this: any study of surviving ministerial correspondence will show things like Robert Cecil, while acting as the King's most influential minister, getting involved in a detailed dispute about the appointment of a schoolmaster at Fotheringay. It is not so very different from the way the minister, in recent times, has become embroiled in the issues raised by the dismissal of a schoolmaster in Lewes. In all centuries, pressure to take things to the top has made it desperately difficult for senior ministers to delegate. If they are ever to have the time and occasional peace needed for taking major decisions of policy, this pressure to take everything to the top must be resisted.

That is why any attempt to preserve a degree of University autonomy must involve self-restraint in Parliament, as well as in ministers, civil servants and Universities. The problem is being recognized in the creation of Next Steps Agencies, in which the minister cannot be held answerable for their daily administration. It is not right, for example, that I should be able to ask the Lord Chancellor questions in Parliament about the conservation of the class of records E 202 in the Public Record Office. The Lord Chancellor has other duties, and other people are better able to judge the state of Exchequer Writs than he is. The plan to turn the Public Record Office into a Next Steps Agency recognizes this. Any such question in future must go where it should have gone before, to the Advisory Council on the Public Records.

The difficulties of the model are illustrated by the Social Security Benefits Agency. It is impossible and unreasonable to restrain members of parliament from raising questions about abuse or misuse of public power which directly affect the well being, and even the being, of their constituents. It is therefore not possible, or reasonable, to stop members of parliament asking questions about the Social Security Benefits Agency. These are then referred to the head of the Benefits Agency, and the replies placed in the library of the relevant House of Parliament. This, however, does not give satisfaction, since others as well as the member of parliament concerned have a legitimate interest in the replies, and there is a growing pressure for the replies to be printed in *Hansard*. This pressure has now been successful.

It is to be hoped, in this area, that Universities are more like the Public Record Office than the Social Security Benefits Agency. Ministers should not be asked questions about the growth of structuralism in the Department of English in the University of X. The difficulty is that the effect of financial stringency is working entirely the other way, and because there is not enough money to go round, University spokesmen are under constant pressure to raise questions about the funding of some specific University service, in order, either to get special protection for it, or to get a general level of funding which allows the University to preserve it. Thus financial stringency is forcing University spokesmen to contradict all their own protests about autonomy, decentralization and academic freedom, and to involve ministers daily more deeply in the conduct of University affairs. While this is the case, there is not much prospect of decentralization in the accountability of Universities. Here there is a link between freedom and funding which will be the central theme of Chapter 3.

There are two other rights resting with the Government in this field which are worth discussion. One is the right to make earmarked grants. These may actually be useful to Universities, by giving protection to a vital service such as library funding from the need to compete with the general clamour for funds. This type of earmarked grant is useful when done in consultation, and to help University authorities to do what they already want to do themselves. It is, though, a power which must be used sparingly, since it is easy to see that it is capable of abuse as well as of use. The use of such powers to remodel the University system in a governmental image would be very dangerous indeed. Such powers are like alcohol: they have a legitimate use, but excessive abuse could lead to demands for prohibition of the legitimate use.

The other type of grant is for a specific earmarked grant for a particular service which the Government wishes to see performed. In the words of Lord Eccles, a former Secretary of State for Education:

> the taxpayer pays such a large part of the Universities' income, and therefore we should be able to say to them from time to time, 'Will you please study this particular subject because it is in the national interest you should?'.[8]

In a working relationship, such a request must be entirely legitimate. The question on which Lord Eccles wanted help was the teaching of mathematics to children. That a Secretary of State should want advice on such a question is no more than natural, and that he should turn to academic sources to get it is something which the academic community can only welcome. Lord Eccles, however, seems to have found some difficulty in getting his advice. If Universities were in a position to give it, and did not, they were to blame. If Governments cannot do this, they will be losing one of the reasons why Governments have wanted Universities ever since the first days of their existence.

On the other hand, people outside Universities do not always appreciate the degree of specialization involved in the ability to do a particular piece of research. It is not enough to be in the right subject: it is necessary to be in the right part of the right subject. For a historian, to take one example, it is necessary, not only to be in the right period, but to be used to working with the right types of source and the right types of question. It is also necessary not to be committed by contractual obligations which may make a publisher's contract as onerous as a mortgage. Granted, then, that this is something Governments have every right to ask, and which they should expect to get, their success in getting it will depend on the existence of a reasonably large research sector in the field. Without that, there may be refusals which look ungracious, but in fact mark a genuine incapacity to do that particular item of research.

Earmarked grants because a Government wants a particular service are one thing. Systematic earmarked grants to change the development of the University sector as a whole are quite another. Here, again, there is a legitimate distinction between use and abuse. Like so much else in the relations between Government and Universities, this is something which depends on trust. If that is absent, no amount of constitutional arrangement will adequately compensate for its absence.

One final way in which English Universities have become inextricably involved with the State is the State's right to grant or withold the power to confer degrees. This is something which is not true in many other countries, for example in the USA. It marks the exceptionally early emergence of a centrally controlled nation state in England: without that emergence, the State simply would not have had the power to make its giving or witholding of approval an effective weapon. In that context, the Universities had as much to do with ensuring that the State acquired this power as anyone else. The State's recognition was important because it was one of the most significant employers of University graduates. For the Universities, the witholding of Crown recognition was a vital weapon in subduing such schismatic rivals as the abortive University of Stamford. It is unlikely to be a coincidence that the royal writ quoted on page 17 above, which described Oxford and Cambridge as 'the King's Universities' was dated the year after the beginning of the Stamford schism.[9] As always, the silence of the document was one of the most interesting things about it: it was saying that Stamford was *not* 'The King's University'.

In some ways, not much has changed in the 654 years between this writ and the Education Bill of 1988. The Government amendment to that bill to tighten up the power to control bogus degrees was widely welcomed by the academics present. The recognition of University degrees confers a particularly valuable form of privilege, and there is no difficulty in seeing why until 1991 it appeared to the Universities to be to their advantage. It is to the advantage of the public, in that it serves to protect them from those who would obtain their money on false pretences, and to the advantage of employers, who need someone to tell them whose degrees they should take seriously. It is also to the advantage of the Government, which, by identifying itself as a vital source of privilege and protection, increases its power and influence in a way as old as Government itself.

On the other hand, any of the more extreme University claims to autonomy must be fatally undermined by the long-standing recognition of this Government power to validate degrees. So long as this power exists, Universities cannot take the extreme autonomist position, that Governments are not entitled to any view on University standards. Governments are taking such a view every time they recognize a graduate as holding the degree of B.A. or B.Sc. It is a more extreme version of the point made by the dependence of the medieval Universities on the Crown to defend their privileges, but in this case, carrying the rider of a right to be concerned with academic standards.

It would be unduly defeatist to upset a relationship which has worked well for some 700 years simply because of what we may hope is a temporary hiccup in trust between the Government and the Universities. It would also be a mistake to upset the arrangement when there is no suitable and generally acceptable alternative in sight. If no one had this power, it would be an open invitation to fraud in a field where there is enough temptation to it already. If the Universities had it themselves, it would serve to strengthen Government suspicions that they are a cartel. If some third body were created to exercise the power, a great new power would be created, and vast arguments would break out over the composition of the body. It would take it a considerable time to gain the instinctive recognition which many centuries have conferred on the existing system.

The lines of solution are in the classic medieval convention for limiting the powers of the Crown: it takes counsel before reaching its decisions, and takes it from those who have the expertise needed to give the relevant advice. In fact, the exercise of the power to validate degrees brings us back, yet again, to the need for some semi-autonomous person or group of people to act as a buffer between Universities and the State. It also brings us back, yet again, to the inextricable interdependence of Universities and the State, and to the fact that no relationship will work long without trust.

3

MAPPING THE BORDERS

It is no part of the Comptroller and Auditor General's duty to question policy decisions reached on academic grounds. His function is to comment and advise on the propriety, regularity and efficiency with which moneys voted by Parliament are administered by those to whom they are entrusted.

> (Rt. Hon. Anthony Crosland, MP, Secretary of State for Education and Science, 26 July 1967)[1]

Ministers are no longer thinking in terms of grants, however calculated, but in terms of buying certain services from Universities . . . The Government is here a single purchaser . . . It will use the power which this situation gives it to press for higher quality and greater efficiency just as Marks and Spencer (for example) does in similar circumstances.

> (Sir Peter Swinnerton-Dyer, last Chairman of the University Grants Committee)[2]

These two quotations illustrate with unusual clarity how Government policy towards the Universities has changed during the 1980s, and why it was felt necessary to reassert the ideal of academic freedom. What has disappeared between the first quotation and the second is the notion of any autonomous sphere of academic judgement. So too has any modest hesitation on the Government's part about its power to judge academic quality. Instead, we have the appearance of the notion of 'efficiency', which, in Government parlance, does not in fact mean doing the job better. A speech touching on the potential conflict between cost-cutting and safety was once described by the minister as having spoken of 'efficiency versus safety'.[3] Efficiency, in the language of this Government, means simply the reduction of unit costs. It is this pressure for 'efficiency', more than anything else, which has created a battleground about the proper limits of the Government's powers.

That Governments should wish to save money is of course perfectly proper. However, they are abusing language in confining the word 'efficiency' to the reduction of unit costs, and leaving no room in the meaning of the word for the ideal of doing the job properly. In the administration of the Social Security Benefits Agency, for example, there is a performance indicator for their success in making decisions accurately. This is as it should be, but it comes as a surprise to laymen to find that they have an entirely *separate* performance indicator for efficiency. 'Efficiency' is nothing to do with making decisions correctly, but only with making them cheaply. This ideal of 'efficiency' is a potential enemy of quality in all our public services. If it can be the enemy of safety on the London Underground, it can be the enemy of scholarship in Universities.

This campaign for 'efficiency' necessarily raises questions about the level on which our public services are managed. The high-level imposition of a priority criterion for decision-making necessarily tends to shift the key influence in making decisions ever further up the scale. Like the Universities under Elizabeth I, Universities under Elizabeth II are being required to manage themselves in accordance with a centrally imposed creed. Simply because this creed is centrally imposed, it must often be imposed, and invoked, in ignorance. It must therefore tend to produce results which are the opposite of those intended. It therefore risks the imposition of a centrally imposed uniformity which is necessarily unresponsive to chronological change or to variations in local situations. It risks indifference to all those manifold situations in which the centrally imposed principle does not work. It reminds me of my father's often expressed indignation at discovering, when he visited Russia in 1920, that during an acute food shortage, Russians were forbidden to catch or eat the fish in the River Moskva. The need to secure public control over the means of production, distribution and exchange took priority over the need to get people something to eat.[4] The central pursuit of 'efficiency', on a lesser scale, carries some of the same risks of a centrally imposed ideology. Power, if it is to be exercised competently, needs to be subject to limits, and Government power to interfere in the detailed running of the public services is no exception. Such interference need not take the form of overriding formal autonomy, and intervening in detailed individual decisions. It may be done just as effectively by the imposition of an overriding general principle.

Nothing is ever going to stop us having Governments with principles, and if these principles are sincerely held, nothing is ever going to prevent Governments from wanting to spread them. The question is about the extent of power with which these principles should be endowed. A parallel question arises in the United States, where, since 1964, Government commitment to the principle of racial equality has influenced its dealings with innumerable spheres of American life. The principle is good, and action in support of it may be good also. Nevertheless, even a good principle raises questions about the limits of Government power when it comes into conflict with another principle. In this case the area of potential conflict is between the principle of racial equality, expressed in the programme of affirmative action, and the principle of appointment by merit, expressed in the normal assumptions of an academic appointing committee. Many of us might wish to support both principles, but this can only be done if it is recognized that there is scope for tension, conflict and adjustment, and even for some argument, between them. It can, for example, be quite difficult to explain to an affirmative-action officer why a committee has not found any Black candidates for a post in English medieval history. It is only if it can be accepted (as in that case it was) that the explanation of such a failure is not *necessarily* in terms of racial discrimination that such a dialogue can even begin. What is essential, when a Government has a principle, is that it should not exist in splendid isolation. It is essential, if principles are to be kept within the bounds of moderation and common sense, that they should not enjoy monopoly. The only thing which can prevent a principle from enjoying arbitrary powers is its collision with another principle. American academics, facing, and usually sympathizing with, the principle of affirmative action, have often been able to control it by the application of the principle of appointment by merit, which is equally deeply embedded in American life, and equally attuned to American values. The result is that the principle of affirmative action has made a steady and controlled progress, normally, so far, without significant erosion of academic standards.[5]

Are British academics, facing the principle of 'efficiency', able to achieve the same feat? Are we too able to invoke a principle, generally accepted in our national life, which is able to provide a check and balance to the principle so vigorously invoked by the Government? It is the purpose of this chapter to suggest that we are, and that the principle on which we should fall back is that decisions should be made by those whose professional training, expertise and knowledge qualifies them to make an informed decision. It is not fundamentally different from the principle on which the Government itself relies in its setting up of Next Steps Agencies. That the decision on what facilities should be provided for the reading of Pipe Rolls is a decision to be taken, with advice, by the Deputy Keeper of Public Records and not by the Lord Chancellor, is a view with which the Government itself does not argue.

This principle is further strengthened in those areas in which the decision depends on a professional skill which the Government does not possess. This is recognized in the management of the National Health Service, in the universally accepted principle that the Government does not make clinical judgements. The decision how quickly patients should be discharged from hospital after an appendectomy, no matter what it may contribute to 'efficiency', is not a proper object of Government policy. The decision whether a particular type of growth requires surgery is one which cannot be a proper object of Government policy. This principle, of course, like all others, has boundary areas, and in these boundary areas there may be boundary disputes. The practice of medicine, like that of scholarship, must necessarily be within the law, and that limitation gives Government, and the courts, a *locus standi* in such areas as that of medical malpractice, but even in those areas where their competence cannot be excluded, Governments take professional advice.

The principle is not based on any belief that medical authorities enjoy professional infallibility. They disagree with each other quite often enough to establish the principle that they are capable of being wrong. The policy that the Government does not make clinical judgements does not rest on any belief that medical judgement is always sound: it rests on a recognition that the Government cannot make it at all. It simply does not enjoy the necessary training and information. While medical authorities may be wrong, Governments probably will be wrong, and if they are right at all, it can only be by coincidence. It is on this understanding that the principle that the Government does not make clinical judgements enjoys universal acceptance.

The contention of this chapter is that it is possible to justify, on very similar grounds, a principle that the Government does not make academic judgements. Such a principle would be rooted in past British practice, and would be very much in line with the restrictions imposed by Mr Anthony Crosland on the Comptroller and Auditor General in 1967. Like the defence of the autonomy of clinical judgement, it would not rest on any claim that academics are always right: there are few vital areas of academic judgement (beyond such basic points as that we must not falsify documents) on which it is not possible to find academics to argue on both sides. The point with academics, as with doctors, is that they must be left to resolve these arguments for themselves. The justification, as with clinical judgement, is that the Government is incompetent to make the judgement itself. This may be no less true if the minister believes, on the strength of undergraduate memories, that he is competent to make it. When the Pope wrote indignantly to the Schools of Paris, complaining that this was not how things were managed when *we* were at the schools, he was merely stating the obvious.[6] He was writing to a University which had changed very greatly in the meantime, partly in response to new currents of scholarship of the very highest long-term significance. If he had been a Regent Master at the Sorbonne, he would have known this in a way, and in a depth, which was not accessible to him as Pope in Rome. The principle is also very similar to that by which ministers do not make operational decisions in warfare: if they do, they will make them wrong, and defeat may well be the result.

Yet even if the fundamental case for the Government's lack of competence were not accepted, there would remain a pragmatic case in terms of the need to get good service. Very few people can work really well in opposition to their primary convictions. Attempts to do so, as those who have studied churchwardens' returns to visitations during the Reformation know very well, tend to result in a token lip-service followed by an evasive formula. If full compliance is exacted by duress, it is not done well. Moreover, full compliance is less easily given in professional matters than it is in more mechanical ones. The tasks of research and teaching, like those of medicine or the law, cannot be done properly without a very considerable degree of dedication, and most people find it difficult to give that degree of dedication to something they believe to be wrong. All professions have their own cultures and codes of values, and if they are deprived of these, they are deprived of that wherein their greatest value to society consists. A doctor ordered to treat fever by bloodletting, or appendicitis by purges, would necessarily perform his task perfunctorily: his heart would not be in it.

The values of professions, of course, are not infallible. They do and should change. What needs to be accepted is the difficulty of changing them by Government action. If the task is done at all, it can only be done through a massive purge, in which many of the best in the profession go abroad. Catholic emigration from Oxford under Elizabeth I, which included no less than 23 Fellows of New College, illustrates the point very well.[7] With a few rapidly promoted exceptions, survivors will tend to be those who care less about their jobs, and that fact is likely to show in how they perform them. Changing the culture of a profession by

Government action, because it is a direct assault on conscience, has something in common with religious persecution. Because it will pre-select those whose conscience is weak in a profession whose operation depends on conscience being strong, it will necessarily lower standards, and perhaps even cast doubt on the profession's claims to survive. Governments which dislike the values of any of the professions must accept their limitations, and rely instead on time and their own allies within the profession. There is thus both a principled and a prudential case in favour of the principle that the Government should not make academic judgements.

If we accept that the Government does not make academic judgements, what are the practical consequences of this principle for relations between Government and Universities? In the first place, it means that Governments cannot judge academic quality. They may legitimately want to know which are the best Universities, but they can neither decide this question for themselves, nor lay down the criteria by which others must do it. The task, if it is to be done at all, must be entirely delegated, and delegated to a largely academic body such as the old University Grants Committee was. If they reply that this is too cosy an arrangement, and tends to make representatives of British Universities judge and party in their own cause, they may have a point to which British academics should pay attention, but it is not the solution to import a large lay membership which will simply not have the compe-tence or the information to make the necessary decisions. Universities, from their very earliest days, have been answerable to an international scholarly community, and it is their judgement which they take ser-iously. If the Government were able to persuade them to undertake the task, the presence of foreign scholars, with different national traditions and different instinctive assumptions, on any body assessing academic standards would be something to which British academics could not object.

What is a great deal less easy to defend is the current use of mechanical and quantifiable 'performance indicators' derived from a Whitehall model whose applicability to University conditions is far from obvious. For example, no one disputes that publication is a legitimate indicator of quality. What most academics are a great deal less easily persuaded of is that one publication is equal to another. The application of such an assumption is likely to favour the academic capable of playing the system, and writing, often with some frequency, the sort of review-type survey of the literature on a subject, which can be tossed off on a Sunday afternoon. Counting this equal with the product of two or three years' archival research, which has shown a central interpretative assumption to be erroneous, is at best misleading. Again, it is difficult to count the substantial archival research which shifts a major assumption as equal with the substantial archival research which merely alters one fact, without any particularly far-reaching significance.

Again, no one disputes that there is a connection between teaching standards and the classes of our pupils' degrees. Yet this is not a direct causal connection, but a relationship full of independent variables, including some, such as the financing of the library, which are more under the Government's control than ours. A severe 'flu epidemic sweeping through a third-year group, or even a defective burglar alarm next door to an examination room, may affect the statistics in ways which are nothing to do with a University's quality. Moreover, except in collegiate Universities such as Oxford, Cambridge and the federal parts of London, examining is normally done by those who do the teaching of the same students. Though there is no suggestion of any lack of integrity in University examining, putting people in charge of manufacturing their own performance indicator in this way creates an unnecessary temptation.

Some performance indicators are based on sheer ignorance, and therefore produce a distortion between subject and subject. For example, the use of success in obtaining outside money as a performance indicator has a significant distorting effect between subject and subject. It may have a distorting effect within one subject between different branches of that subject. In history, for example, it will tend to favour foreign at the expense of British history, and no one who remembers the debates on history in the National Curriculum is likely to believe that this effect was intended: it must be the result of ignorance. A British historian, especially if based in or near London, may be able to keep up a very substantial research output without needing more money than salaried time. He may be able to teach in the morning and research in the afternoon, and for that type of activity, no outside money is needed. A historian of Spain, on the other hand, will not be able to complete serious projects without long periods of time in the archives at Simancas and elsewhere. It is not possible to pop into Simancas after attending a morning meeting in one's department. It is necessary to travel, and to secure accommodation away from home, and these activities require grants. The 'performance indicator' of success in obtaining outside money will thus say that a historian of Spain is much better than an equally competent historian of England: the historian of Scotland will come somewhere in between, unless he is based north of the Border.

Similarly, the reliance on outside money as an indicator will favour economic and social history, to which large quantitative projects with sophisticated computer equipment may be appropriate, at the expense of the historian of ideas, who needs only to travel to the British Library to read Plato, Mill or Marx. Since every small department is a statistically insignificant sample, results may be seriously distorted by the presence (or absence) of one historian engaged in a field to which large grants of outside money are appropriate. Since it is very hard to believe that its operation is the result of deliberate purpose, it tends to illustrate the principle that outside authorities lack the competence to make academic judgements.

The principle would also tend to show that politicians cannot be adequate judges of University entrance qualifications. The purpose of an entrance qualification is not only one of competitive selection, but also to provide evidence that the candidate is capable of doing the work. The Government's contribution to fixing criteria for entrance must be considerable for the first criterion, but nil for the second. Competitive selection must depend on the total numbers admitted, and since Government foots the bill, it must be capable of putting an upper ceiling on numbers admitted. If this were not so, it would be being asked to write the sort of blank cheque which only natural-rights theory can defend, and which no national economy can sustain. It is Government's right to say it will pay for the admission of a certain number of undergraduates, and, granted a reasonable flexibility at the margins, Universities should not expect them to pay for any more.

On the other hand, no department can be required to fill a specified number of places unless it can find people capable of doing the work. What evidence may be taken to indicate that a candidate is capable of doing the work is entirely a question for the Universities. They know what the work is, and they know what skills are required to do it. The question of what should be taken as evidence of those skills is a question of practical experience, and to require Universities to take in people they believe incapable of doing the work is an abuse of academic freedom. This has been made manifest in some of the open enrolment programmes which have come in in the United States since the 1960s, in which it has not been unknown for University teachers to spend their time teaching their pupils to read.[8] That people should be taught to read at the public expense is no doubt a worthwhile use of public money, but there is room for doubt whether the resultant qualification is properly called a degree. It is a little like employing an RAF test pilot to teach people to ride a bicycle. This means, then, that if Universities are not satisfied with the reforms of A Level examinations we are encouraged in many quarters to expect, they are entirely entitled to go back to having their own entrance examinations, and to awarding their places on the results of these examinations. The use of A Level as a University selector has always owed more to academics' desire to keep down the number of hours they spend interviewing than to any appropriateness it may have as a University entrance examination. Any attempt to reform it must rest on the acceptance that Universities cannot be forced to require any qualification by which they are not intellectually convinced, nor to refrain from requiring one by which they are. In fact, any reform of A Levels must be based on the assumption that the State does not prescribe University entrance qualifications, and on the further assumption that the school leaving qualification and the University entrance qualification need not be identical.

By the same logic, Governments have no standing in saying what the standard of the degree should be. This, in any case, is not purely a national matter, and should not come under any single national control. From the earliest years of degrees, they have been valued because they were taken to confer the *ius ubique docendi*, the right to teach anywhere. It is part of the value of a University degree that it should enjoy international recognition. This fact means that no one country can afford to impose unilateral variations on the standard of its degrees, without putting its graduates at a grave disadvantage in other countries. Indeed, if a country's own degrees are devalued too far for international recognition, it risks creating the equivalent of a hard-currency market in the degrees of other countries. Since undergraduates tend to be of an age at which there is more freedom to travel than there often is for those younger or older, there tends to be something of an international free market in degrees. It is, of course, not to be maintained that every University in the world always manages to maintain its degrees at an exact common standard: some slippage inevitably creeps in. Yet so long as there is enough student travel to keep up something of a free market in degrees, it is capable of reacting to these slippages. One of the revelations of the Gulf War, to many people, was the number of Iraqi students in this country. It would be a fair deduction from this that degrees from, say, London carry a higher prestige than degrees from Baghdad. A country which has, as it were, a hard-currency degree would be extremely unwise to abandon it for the short-term benefits of competitive devaluation. Since Universities are international communities, and gain much of their intellectual value from this fact, they tend, apart from intrinsic ability to judge the qualifications, to be much more alert to these ebbs and flows than any Government, responsible only for one country, can ever be. Such perceptions are built up by a series of exchanges by word of mouth. Once, when I had spoken to a sixth-form conference, I was asked to advise a sixth former who was sitting on offers of a place from both Oxford and Yale. I advised her that these offers were, in academic terms, equal, and the degrees they offered of equal value. Should it become necessary to answer this question in a different way, this country would suffer a very significant loss.

If Universities, in this country and abroad, are the sole competent judges of the standard of our degrees, it follows that it is beyond the Government's competence to judge how long a degree should take. Occasional Government suggestions of moves to a two-year degree are beyond the limits of their competence, and an interference with academic judgement. Curiously, there has so far been no serious attempt to shorten the Scottish four-year degree. The unsuccessful attempt to insert a clause in the Further and Higher Education Bill to allow the Government to shorten the length of degree courses was confined to the English bill. The absence of an equivalent clause in the Scottish bill may indicate a successful resistance by St Andrew's House to Whitehall. If so, it is another example of the principle that a degree of autonomy has constitutional value. Academic freedom plus Scottish law may have achieved a victory which neither could have achieved singly. The Government should also bear in mind that our present three-year degree is already shorter than any of its significant competitors. Most, like the Americans, require four years, and the Germans a very great deal longer. The English degree (not the British, since Scottish degrees already require four years) is thus already under significant pressure in keeping up its standard while taking a shorter time than anyone else. This has hitherto been possible because of the acceptance that University vacations, for undergraduates as well as for staff, were periods very largely designed for the sort of intensive academic work which cannot be fitted into a weekly teaching timetable. The Government should also bear in mind that this three-year degree has made things very much cheaper for it than they could possibly have been otherwise. They ought, also, to quote figures, when they attempt international comparisons of costs, of the total cost of producing a graduate, and not of the cost per annum. Figures of the cost per annum have a built-in bias of 25 per cent against England. If pincer pressure on the length of the degree and on academic use of vacations should be kept up, the strain on the standard of the degree would be more than it could take. There is a story which used to be told in Oxford of a man from the University of Albuquerque (New

Mexico), who wanted to do postgraduate work in Oxford. He was given an interview, and was asked the source of his degree. He replied 'Albuquerque', and saw the interviewer write down what, seen from upside down, looked remarkably like 'no degree'. This, no doubt, was a piece of Oxford arrogance, but for that very reason, we should fear that if Albuquerque is ever given the opportunity to return the compliment, it will find it irresistible.

If it is entirely a matter for Universities to determine the standard of the degree, it must also be entirely a matter for Universities to decide how much work is necessary to be competently prepared for the examination. That, surely, perhaps more than anything else, is a matter of academic judgement, and Governments simply do not have the authority to intervene in it. They do not know, and cannot prescribe, what books it is necessary to read, what lectures it is necessary to attend, or what essays it is necessary to write. Indeed, academics themselves would not presume to prescribe such things for any subject but their own. Such subjects as Chemistry at Oxford, which say they require four years to reach an acceptable standard, put themselves at a competitive disadvantage by doing so, but their assertion is one which, as a historian, I lack the competence to challenge.

This means that Governments lack the authority to refuse to recognize the need for undergraduates to work in vacations. They cannot pretend that the whole body of required work can be done during term-time when academics tell them otherwise. The ministerial assertion that 'it is a matter for the individual student to determine when he does his studying. Some students will study in vacations',[9] while couched in the language of individual autonomy, was an interference with the autonomy of the Universities, and an interference with an academic judgement that the amount of work required is greater than it is possible to complete during nine terms. Ministers have no more authority to tell Universities that they cannot require students to work in vacations than academics have to tell ministers that they cannot require civil servants to be at their desks during the parliamentary recess. In both cases, it is those who are in the field who are competent to judge the amount of work required. If ministers should choose to say that undergraduates cannot be financed during vacations, they must accept the academic counter-argument that the degree must then take four years. If they ask us for a different pattern of organization because it is easier for them to finance, that is a legitimate matter for negotiation. What is not legitimate is fixing the amount of work required for a degree by ministerial decision. That is an interference with academic freedom.

This same principle, that it is for the Universities to determine the amount of work needed for a degree, must imply the right of Universities to say that undergraduates must be full-time during term, and must not take other paid employment. Again, there is scope for negotiation if the Government should ask us to space work out differently, and allow a four-year degree on a part-time basis. That would be a legitimate matter for negotiation, and though Universities might not welcome such a change, it could be defended within the limits of academic freedom, because it would not necessarily be a threat to the standard of the degree. It is an altogether different matter when a minister says, within the context of the existing three-year degree, that 'I doubt whether any single College in this country can ban a student from taking paid work either inside or outside of term time.'[10] This is an interference in the contractual relationship between a University and its students such as would not be tolerated between a private firm and its employees. It is also, once again, an assumption of direct authority over the amount of work required to get a degree, and that assumption of authority is beyond the scope of the Government's competence. It is on a level with telling doctors how quickly patients should be discharged from hospital after an appendectomy.

The same arguments apply to current Government attempts to lay down the length of time a Ph.D. must take. For them to say they provide funding only for a certain number of years, and that postgraduates who fail to complete in that time do so at their own risk, is within their rights. What is not within their rights is to make the academic judgement that a piece of research must be completed in a certain space of time. That is a judgement no academic has the right to make for another, and it is one the Government has no competence to make for any of us. The present system, where Ph.D.s not completed after four years are classified as not completed (even if they are completed to universal acclaim rather later), and the postgraduate's college loses funds as a result, is absolutely the paradigm case of the pursuit of 'efficiency' threatening academic standards and interfering with academic judgement.

The Ph.D. is not a course: it is a piece of research. The only person who can judge what is necessary to a piece of research is the researcher. Even the researcher cannot do it before beginning: it is part of the definition of research that you do not know what you are going to find out. It is those who make big and unexpected discoveries, or who are forced by the evidence to change the preconceptions they began with, who tend to take longest, and it is therefore often the best postgraduates who, along with their Colleges, are most severely penalized. It is no use saying that the conclusions can be submitted in an interim form, and worked up more fully afterwards: the question is whether the conclusions are themselves true, and the real evil of the time limit is the extent to which it forces people to make up their minds on that question before they have done the research on which a decision should be based. As every minister who has announced a new policy in the face of an opposition censure motion knows, it is very difficult, once one has nailed one's colours to the mast in defence of a position, to convince oneself thereafter that it was mistaken. It is in this way that the time limit produces research which will not meet the test of the pursuit of knowledge for its own sake.

The Ph.D., even more than the B.A. or the B.Sc., exists in an international market, and must be capable of commanding international recognition. It is thus very difficult, and very unwise, for one country to introduce a unilateral devaluation of its Ph.D., for it will put its own candidates at a disadvantage on the international job market. It is probably true today that more British Ph.D.s get academic jobs outside Britain than inside it, and if they come to discover that the bargaining power of their Ph.D. is diminished because it is British, they will, if they can raise the money by hook or by crook, look for a Ph.D. in another country.

The Government would be entirely within its rights if it withdrew funding for the Ph.D. altogether: no University, and no degree, enjoys any natural right to Government funding. What they are not entitled to do is to impose an arbitrary and unilateral change in the standard, not calculated for any academic reasons or justified on any academic grounds. The present policy, by tempting people to tailor their findings to fit a time limit, is an invitation to scholarly dishonesty.

Where the present policy has perhaps achieved a useful effect, even if only by accident, is in exposing the existence of a very wide difference between the standard of the Ph.D. in one subject and another. Two Ph.D.s in history in London and in Berkeley probably enjoy a clearer common standard with each other than either has with a Ph.D. in Chemistry in the same University. We are often told that the time limit is comparatively unimportant because the Ph.D. is only a research training. This may be a valid argument in some subjects, but there are others, of which history is one, in which the only way to acquire a research training is by doing a piece of research and taking it through to completion. It is in these subjects that the effect of the present policy is particularly severe.

It would also follow from accepting a principle that Governments do not make academic judgments that they have no authority to prescribe teaching methods. We are often told at the moment that we ought to be moving over to 'modular courses', a course-unit based approach which allows undergraduates to put together a degree à la carte, rather than following the menu laid down in a set syllabus. This is something on which academic opinion itself is deeply divided, and it is not possible to claim to make a case against it in the name of 'academic opinion'. What I think it is possible to argue is that the question is one which should be resolved by academics themselves, rather than having it settled by means of Government inducements. The motives for which politicians ask us to undertake this change are not bad ones, even from a strictly academic point of view. They want it to be easier for people to do degrees on a part-time basis or by instalments, rather than having to take three full-time years in a row. There is nothing wrong with the objective, and those familiar with Birkbeck College or the Open University, to say nothing of the great Universities of the United States, must admit that it is compatible with the achievement of high standards.

Yet there are problems about this approach. It conflicts with the equally laudable desire, apparent in the planning of the National Curriculum for schools, to provide a basic grounding which anyone educated in the subject should know something about. A course-unit or modular education must make it possible to take a First-class degree in history without ever having heard of Luther, or of Karl Marx. It makes it possible to get a First-class degree while concentrating entirely on one sort of history. It would be possible, if enough options were available, to be successful while having worked only on medieval history, or women's history. It would make it possible to get a good degree while taking courses only from Marxist (or anti-Marxist) professors, or taking them only from men (or from women). It is possible to argue that this risks leaving people without the context needed to understand what they do.

It is also true that it creates problems with examining. In the system of the traditional English syllabus, every teacher has to prepare his pupils to be examined by someone else. In London (the federal parts), Oxford and Cambridge, the teacher does not know who this will be. This imposes on the teacher a discipline of need to cover other aspects of the subject than that on which he is stirred to enthusiasm. It forces the most missionary teacher to familiarize his pupils with the approaches of those with whom he disagrees most passionately. The examining system thus imposes a duty of impartiality on the teacher.

In a course-unit or modular system, on the other hand, the teacher will be sovereign over the examining of his own courses. In the English system, the papers he marks will be marked by a second marker. Yet if he is teaching on medieval marriage doctrines, or the history of Senegal, it is doubtful whether the second marker will know very much about the subject. He will spot any visible and gross bias, but he will probably not know if whole interpretations of the field have been simply ignored. In America, where the institution of the second marker, and of the external examiner, is hardly known, the professor has complete sovereign power over his teaching, and, through his teaching assistants, over his examining. Anyone who has listened to American undergraduates talking frankly to each other over lunch will have heard them tell each other: 'If you think that, don't say it in Professor X's course: you won't get a good grade for it: he can't stand it.' For the professor himself, the knowledge that he enjoys a complete arbitrary power to indulge his biases as far as he likes creates a temptation which is not always easy to resist.

These objections are not necessarily insuperable, but they deserve consideration. They are ones which busy politicians, with issues coming at them like West Indian fast bowling, will not necessarily think of for themselves. It is possible that some supporters of modular courses at Westminster, if they were aware of these issues, might wish to change their minds. Granted that this is an issue on which points can be made on both sides, it may still be fair to argue that it is not the type of decision which ought to be made by politicians. The fact that academic judgement is divided does not make the issue any less a matter of academic judgement.

Equally, politicians should get over the hankering they have had ever since the 1960s to interfere with the pattern of the academic year. They ought to be better able to appreciate this point than they are, since they live in the same glass house. The parliamentary recess is necessary for exactly the same reason as the Long Vacation: without it, no one would ever succeed in doing any work. For a politician, the danger of slipping into an ephemeral approach, in which the issues of the moment blot out the underlying themes behind them, is always present. It is something of which they are often enough accused, and which most of them fear. If they did not have time in the recess to read, to travel, and simply to think, the standard of their performance would be very much lower than it is. Equally, if ministers did not have quiet spells at their desks, not interrupted by parliamentary Questions, organized deputations, three-line whips and so forth, their bills would be much worse prepared even than they are. Academics often come up with rational plans for reorganizing Westminster. These are often superbly argued, and sound entirely convincing, but they simply do not rest on a practical awareness of how the system works. Politicians ought to remember how they feel about such proposals before they try to tinker with the University year. The ones who are tempted to assume that academics are not working when they are not teaching ought to remember their feelings about those of their own constituents who believe they were not working because they were not in the Chamber last time it was televised. Above all, they ought to cease attacking the Long Vacation unless they are prepared to abandon the parliamentary recess.

Most serious academic research gets done in the Long Vacation, and anyone discussing a publication timetable with a publisher will know that they have learnt to measure timetables to completing in terms of the number of Long Vacations. Some, but not all, of us manage to continue an established line of research during term, but almost none of us can get a new line of research under way except during the Long Vacation. Without it, the contractual obligation to do research would be almost unenforceable, and those academics to whom research is a vocation (normally the best of the profession) would rapidly begin a search for jobs in other countries. In these terms, the Long Vacation is equally necessary for undergraduates, who cannot hope to undertake tasks like the 1,200 pages or so of reading in original texts needed to get a special subject under way at any other time of the academic year. The organization of the academic year is a by-product of the length of time different types of work take. Organizing it is essentially a matter of academic judgement, and beyond politicians' competence, just as it is beyond academics' competence to reorganize the political year.

The Government at present believes it is entitled to determine the balance between subjects in Universities. The Lord Chancellor argued that:

> if the University received money on the basis that it has courses in Sanskrit, Arabic and pure mathematics, I hope it would be understood that it would provide those courses, and that it would not give the money to philosophy, politics or something else.[11]

In the short term, he has a fair point. This, however, is a field in which the power both of Governments and of Universities is limited. This is for essentially free-market reasons. Subjects come and go for reasons which are very hard indeed to predict. For example, no one in 1988 anticipated the revival in Classics, and even in classical languages, which is now reported to be under way. It is difficult to argue that the number of places available in a subject should be entirely unconnected with the number of people who want to read it. Even if such a position were defended in theory, it could be very difficult to sustain in practice.

The reasons for the rise and fall in the popularity of subjects are not entirely whims of fashion, but may also represent how far those subjects are in a healthy intellectual state, and how far they are at the cutting edge of the movement of ideas. It would, for example, be equally dangerous to freeze the numbers in Social Science departments either at the high point they reached in the 1960s, or at the low point they reached in the 1980s. Demand is by no means an infallible guide to the intellectual value of a subject, but it is no more inaccurate than the predictions of planners, whether academic or governmental. If ideas are not to get set in institutional amber, there should be some give and take between planning predictions and and the fluctuations of demand. If the Government can foresee a particular shortage of a certain type of trained manpower, such as doctors, chemists or engineers, it is entirely justified in asking Universities to meet it. Yet, since forecasts based on manpower planning are almost always wrong, this should be done with a certain caution. Some leeway must be left to Universities to meet the principles of supply and demand. If this is not done, an ossified intellectual structure will be created, and quality will consequently fall.

Equally, it is necessary to appreciate the need to keep up a research base in fields which do not immediately seem urgent. In 1981, no one anticipated the calls on scientific manpower which are made by the spread of AIDS. It is necessary to remember the time-lag which follows from the decision to build up a subject to the creation of a serious research team. Someone has to be appointed to lead it, and he must take on postgraduates, if the undergraduate training exists to produce those qualified to do postgraduate work in the field. It is not until those postgraduates are training postgraduates of their own, which may be some ten or fifteen years, that an adequate team will be in place. Since it is usually not until a crisis has been in progress for some years that it is possible to get money out of the Treasury to meet it, reviving a field which has been allowed to run down may take as much as twenty years. In a fast-moving scientific field, in which an opportunity only needs to appear for people in twenty countries to go for it, this sort of planning will leave us always behind the game.

Much the same arguments apply to the efforts which were being made in the late 1980s to run down and to close departments of Russian. By 1989, it was apparent that this had been a mistake, and the Wooding

Report provided a programme for putting it right. Yet the Wooding Report will not be yielding lively results until well into the next century. Meanwhile, we have a severe shortage of academics, either to advise us on the significance of changes which may affect our policy for a century or more, or to provide our firms with people capable of speaking the language of what may be one of the biggest new markets to open up in a very long time. The Americans, who keep a much larger research base, have certainly not made the same mistake, and they may steal both a political and a commercial march on us as a result.

No one maintains that academics are better able to foresee these things than other people. The Universities cannot claim to have anticipated the collapse of communism more accurately than the Foreign Office. What can be claimed here is that some attention to the principle of selection on merit, and therefore some attention to the principle of supply and demand, may provide a vital degree of flexibility in meeting such unexpected events. It is also fair to claim that some protection for 'unworldly subjects' (which Russian was certainly thought to be in 1987) may turn out to be an unexpected blessing when the world changes with the unpredictability it usually shows. The planning of the balance of academic subjects is as risky as other forms of economic planning, and ought to be done with a due regard for the probability of error.

Few forms of academic freedom are more central than the freedom to choose research topics. Indeed, without that freedom, the freedom to publish 'controversial or unpopular' opinions is likely to be a dead letter. Government control by blocking off some topics of enquiry, because it does not involve the headline-making interference incident to any attempt to censor research already done, is far the easier method of controlling lines of intellectual enquiry. There is no need to impute a desire to censor: those senior enough to be in a position to take decisions on research topics tend to be those with good work behind them, who naturally have a vested interest in believing it to have been correct. Their judgement of what is a 'significant' research topic is likely to be influenced by the academic climate of some ten to fifteen years earlier. They may, then, with the fullest respect for academic freedom, dismiss something as 'a very boring subject', when in fact it opens up big new questions urgently in need of discussion.

There is, of course, no suggestion of the Government prescribing research topics. It takes years of experience in most fields even to know what has been done already, let alone to identify significant new questions. There is no suggestion of Governments having the sort of contempt for academic freedom which would lead them to set out to prescribe lines of research for themselves. Academics also are usually extremely sensitive to the dangers of directing research. There is one very rare story told of a Head of Department who told a junior lecturer what to research on. Fortunately, this was in the palmy days of the 1960s, when there was still a job market which permitted mobility. The lecturer in question simply applied immediately for a job elsewhere, and got it, to universal applause.

Yet, though there seems to be no bad intention in this area, there are dangers of accidental damage. The first, and less serious, arises from the determination of the Government to shift a large part of the money it grants for research away from the budgets of the Universities concerned, and into the budgets of the research councils. This means that, instead of receiving research money as part of his salary, and having terms and conditions of service which allow him time to do research, an academic will have to apply to a research council for a grant. This would mean that the grant would finance leave of absence, and the hiring of a deputy to do the teaching while the research is in progress. The change seems to follow from Government pressure to worsen the staff–student ratio, and, though it is clearly designed to save money, may end up costing more to achieve the same effect.

The result of this change will inevitably be to lessen the researcher's area of autonomy, in which he has a completely sovereign choice of research topic. Instead, it will increase the area in which research cannot be done unless a research council can be convinced it is worthwhile. There are, of course, some subjects in which such a development is inevitable, because of the capital-intensive character of the research involved. Research on the ozone layer, for example, necessarily involves the sort of equipment which cannot be financed without a grant. On the other hand, in the cottage industry subjects, such as Philosophy, English or History, the cost of research is simply that of the lecturer's time. The cost of the research to the lecturer will be measured in shoe-leather and tube fares, notebooks and typewriter ribbons, which he will normally be expected to meet out of his own pocket. In these circumstances, all that is needed to allow the lecturer to do research is a teaching load limited enough to allow him the time. It is in these fields that there is no need at all for any interference with the autonomy of the academic's choice of research topic. There is no need for it to fit the fashions of those who happen to be nominated to the relevant research council, and no need for output to languish if the scholar's assumptions happen to be out of fashion. If this change had been in place over the past twenty years, it would have severely handicapped monetarist economists in the 1970s, and Keynesian economists in the 1980s. For anyone who believes that it is the function of prevailing orthodoxies to be attacked, it might have seemed more appropriate to have it the other way round.

Another unintended threat may reside in the current fashion for encouraging Universities to fund their research by hiring it out on contract to outside bodies who may want to hire their staff to do it. Few, if any, academics would be so fundamentalist as to want to forbid contract research altogether. However, rather more academics might regard it in the same light as writing books such as this one: a secondary activity, not to be taken as part of the scholar's main record of achievement. This is because contract research must necessarily carry some risks to the researcher's autonomy, and because therefore the suspicion must exist that the research will not always be as good as research conducted with full academic freedom.

In the first place, contract research must be undertaken to answer someone else's questions. This is not always a bad thing: no mind is at its best for long in solitude, and the questions may themselves stimulate the scholar's imagination. Yet, because they are questions a non-academic has already thought of, they must often be questions which are not at the cutting edge of research. So long as contract research is undertaken in a context in which 'blue skies' research is the normal pattern, the one will rub off on the other, and not much harm will be done. If contract research should ever become the normal pattern, however, we would be in a very different world indeed. Just to take a few famous names, Archimedes, Copernicus, Galileo, Harvey and Mendel would have been unlikely ever to find funding for their research on a contract basis, because their ideas were unfashionable or unpopular at the time they did their research. The idea of Socrates doing contract research would be a rich subject for comedy. Contract research cannot become the basic bread and butter of academic research without an implied threat to academic freedom.

Indeed, without a substantial group of people engaged in the pursuit of knowledge for its own sake, there will often be no services available for the contractor to buy. It is most unlikely that twenty years ago, manufacturers of refrigerators or fire extinguishers saw any reason for commercial interest in research on the upper atmosphere. If there had not been a group of people pursuing knowledge of the upper atmosphere for its own sake, they would never have known that they had any need to take a commercial interest in these questions. Had they discovered the fact because of research done in other countries, they would not have had any home-based researchers to turn to when they needed them.

There is further ground for misgiving in the fact that any researcher who sells his services to an outside buyer necessarily acquires obligations to something other than the pursuit of knowledge for its own sake. It is not necessary, for this to be the case, for the employer to exert any improper pressure. Since academics are no better than other people, they are capable, as others are, of fearing to endanger a source of income by producing unwelcome findings. Some years ago, when the price of gold was particularly high, a group of bankers formed a consortium to dive for gold in sunken wrecks. They very sensibly employed a young maritime historian to report to them on the likely cargoes of wrecks for which they considered diving. The maritime historian, given a trial contract for one wreck, discovered a full inventory of its cargo, and reported that under no circumstances should they dive for this wreck. Its cargo consisted only of pepper, and their chance of covering their costs was nil. A number of his friends told him that he had been extremely foolish to threaten his prospects of employment by giving such an unwelcome report. Fortunately, the bankers took the intelligent view of the matter, and were very grateful to have been spared useless expense. However, the story does illustrate the temptations to which contract researchers are subject, and the case of thalidomide, among many others, reminds us of the harm which may be done. This need not be a matter of falsifying findings. Everyone who has read any document emanating from Whitehall knows that, without the least untruth, it is possible to present findings in a positive or a negative light. The same is true of research. Because contract research gives rise to temptation, it is essential that it should be done in an intellectual climate dominated by the pursuit of knowledge for its own sake. If this is not so, the contractor will be less likely to get something worth paying for. It is, then, essential to academic freedom that the University atmosphere should be dominated by those who choose their research topics for no other motive but the pursuit of knowledge for its own sake. Like Test cricketers, they must supply the pattern which others seek to emulate.

The misgivings about contract research are, of course, no less when the contractor is the Government itself. This is why there is a potential, if not actual, threat to academic freedom in the new insertion in research contracts for the Departments of Health and Social Security, prohibiting publication without the consent of the Secretary of State. Freedom to publish has for a long time been taken as one of the touchstones of academic freedom. It is the fact of publication which exposes research to the judgement of our professional peers. However expert the research may be, it is only if it has been exposed to that judgement and survived it that we have any good reason to believe it is true. It is also a fundamental academic value, and one in necessary conflict with commercial values, that ideas and findings must be shared with fellow scholars, and become part of our common professional stock-in-trade. It is also the ability to publish which is the acid test of how far the research is under the control of the researcher. It is how far the research is under the control of the researcher which will be one of the touchstones used by the academic world in deciding whether it accepts the research as true.

It is worrying that the Government should defend this situation by invoking the rights of the employer at common law.[12] They are of course correct about what those rights are. The output of an employee is the property of his employer, and the employer may enjoy the intellectual property resulting from the work. However, invoking this doctrine in support of the right to refuse publication to the research seems to indicate a misapprehension. It indicates a mistaken notion of how far an employer may 'own' the output of an academic without making the output in question cease to be that of an academic. Research which is undertaken without freedom to follow the argument where it may lead, and without freedom to share the results with fellow academics, risks being not fully academic work. It risks lowering the academic to the status of a sort of 'hired gun', at the disposal of his employer. If this is so, he is no longer engaged in the pursuit of knowledge for its own sake, and what the employer is getting is something a good deal less than genuine research. Again, this is not only a matter of the risk of false findings. It is perfectly possible for someone hoping for publication to succumb to the temptation to present his findings in a certain light, perhaps even without knowing that he has done so. This is a risk of which Government is insufficiently aware. In March 1988, the Secretary of State wrote to the Chairman of the Committee of Vice-Chancellors and Principals claiming that the old contract had left the Secretary of State with little or no 'control' over the use of the research work.[13] In saying this, he was complaining of that which made it genuine research work. It is not the task of the contractor for research to 'control' the work: if he does, he diminishes its quality, and deprives himself of reasons to believe that it is true. Any claim to 'control' over research work, however modestly it is exercised, is necessarily an infringement of academic freedom. Any argument which asserts otherwise misunderstands the nature of academic work itself.

This is not to assert that there are no circumstances in which leave to publish may be denied. Any claim to publication must rest on ability to demonstrate that the work is of sufficient quality, and that demonstration must be to the satisfaction of someone other than the researcher. Academics are not entitled to be judge and party in their own cause when the quality of their own work is at issue. It is perfectly reasonable to suggest, as the Government has done, that publication should be restricted in cases involving libel, breach of confidentiality and factual error. The issue of libel is a matter of freedom within the law, which is the only freedom any of us are entitled to claim. Confidentiality, especially in the Social Sciences, where so many of the examples used must be case studies of living people, is likely to be a necessarily implied condition of doing the research, and is in the nature of a contractual obligation on the researcher. Factual error will call in question the academic status of the research, and therefore its fitness for publication. It must also be accepted, in cases involving defence research, that publication may be inhibited by the Official Secrets Act. Such restrictions have created a lot of debate in American Universities about how far academics may engage in defence research. There is a case for having such research done by scientists permanently employed by the defence authorities, whose obligations may be less likely to come into conflict with their professional duties. In a good relationship between Government and Universities, there may be no need for the taking of fundamentalist positions on individual cases. This can only be so if freedom to publish is recognized as an academic freedom, and the normal condition of research contracts except when there are compelling individual reasons why it should be otherwise.

4

UNIT COSTS

Being cost-effective does not necessarily mean giving a better, but rather a more efficient, service.

(Rt. Hon. John Moore, MP,
Secretary of State for Social Security)[1]

This distinction is at the very heart of this Government's thinking on all the public services, and the Universities are no exception. By making public services more efficient, they mean reducing their unit costs, and either providing the same amount of services for less money, or providing more services for the same amount of money. In Universities, it has meant a fall of 12 per cent since 1981 in the amount of money per student. This fall is continuing. In the case of the health service, the objective, as the present Prime Minister Mr Major put it at a press conference in the spring of 1991, is to provide more health care per pound. Similarly, the objective of 'efficiency' in higher education, enunciated almost daily in Government statements, is a desire to provide more education per pound.

There is an obvious possibility of conflict between this objective and the more traditional service objective of providing a better quality service. As Lord Grimond once put it, the preaching of 'efficiency' 'gives the impression, which I am sure is wrong, that the Government might regard a worse public service as being cost-effective'.[2] As always with such attempts to pursue a creed, the caricature, while remaining a caricature, may be particularly valuable in revealing the inwardness of the policy, and the caricature may come from someone well below the highest level. Mr Mark Baker, chief executive of Bradford Hospital, one of the new National Health Service (N.H.S.) trusts, recently observed that success in marketing clinical services to customers should become the benchmark for judging N.H.S. hospital performance, rather than ability to cure them. He underlined his point with macabre dedication by saying: 'whether or not patients get better is, in any case, a matter of perception that is not always backed by objectivity. The biggest dona-tions to the health service come from relatives of the deceased.'[3]

Few, if any, Government spokesmen are this frank about the poten-tial conflict between the new public-service ideology and the old, still less about the need to give primacy to one over the other. Yet in logic it must be admitted that the two ideals are capable of conflicting. This, in itself, is not wrong, and could even be helpful. It is not always justifiable to provide the very best service possible, regardless of cost. A minister who is capable of introducing a measure which will save a single life per year at a cost of £1 billion a life is not therefore under a duty to do it. If this were recognized as a duty, the saving of some 200 lives a year would take up the whole of the Government's budget, and it would take some imagination to work out what would happen to the lives which re-mained. Other things being equal (and the qualification is vital), reducing costs is a legitimate, and indeed a necessary, objective. The number of places in which a Government can say that money is no object is necessarily limited, and for every one in which it does, it must refuse to do so in many others.

This is perhaps one of the cases discussed above in which it is good that a principle should come into conflict with another principle. Yet, if the tension necessarily involved is to be kept healthy and creative, it is necessary that neither of these principles should be lost sight of. This means that neither should be given automatic priority over the other. Academics cannot claim the automatic right to draw cheques on the public purse, regardless of other commitments, and Governments cannot claim an automatic right to impose 'efficiency', regardless of the effect on quality of service. It would, for example, immeasurably raise the standard of education in this country if every University possessed a copyright library, yet however much academics might hanker after such a situation, we must accept that it would be a luxury. This, essentially, is because it is not necessary to keeping up with our international competitors: it is not part of University standards round the world, and a University can perfectly well be recognized as up to standard without it.

It is hard to see how the necessary tension can be achieved if one ideal is given statutory primacy over the other. In the Education Reform Bill, the clause setting up the University Commissioners to review University statutes had a purpose clause requiring the Commissioners to 'have regard to the need . . . to enable qualifying institutions to . . . engage in research efficiently and economically'.[4] There was no balancing phrase about the need to enable qualifying institutions to do research well. The identity of the University Commissioners caused no complaint, but since, in the nature of their duties, they were a body dominated by lawyers, their capacity to judge how far research in Physics was done 'efficiently and economically' was necessarily limited. There was no protection in the wording of the clause against Lord Grimond's hypothetical case of the worse service which is regarded as most cost-effective.

Such purpose clauses are becoming normal in Government legislation. There was a very similar clause in the Water Bill, putting an obligation on the new private water companies to provide water efficiently and economically. An attempt was made to amend the Bill to put in a balancing phrase to insert a duty to ensure the quality of water, but the Government resisted this amendment vigorously. It does not take much imagination, then, to see that the pursuit of 'efficiency' is capable of offering a threat to standards of scholarship, of health care and of water, to mention only a few. If the necessary creative tension is to be achieved, a countervailing principle must be asserted.

This is not intended to deny that there is a shortage of money. There is perhaps some substance in the Thatcherite view that this country has built up a larger body of public services than it is able to afford, and nothing is a more powerful way of arguing this view than to ask an opposition politician to sit down and cost the amount of money needed to restore those services to a proper level of quality. Yet it is the characteristic weakness of the political profession that their eyes are bigger than their stomachs. Because they always want, for perfectly good reasons, to do more than they can afford to pay for, they end up under acute pressure to do things on the cheap, and therefore to inadequate standards. The way the Public Expenditure round has been conducted, by a series of bilateral bargains, tends to have the same effect, of allowing each minister to end up with half the money he requested, when it might have been much better for the quality of service for some to end up with all of the extra money they asked for, and the rest to have to manage with none until the next year. The political difficulties of such a proposal are as clear as its administrative advantages. Yet they have been overcome in the 1992 Public Spending round.

Politicians, then, must learn to resist the temptation to go on and on spreading their money thinner, in order that none of them should be utterly disappointed. What they should never do is what Mr Kenneth Baker did, and combine the assertion that it is not imaginable that any Government of any political persuasion will substantially increase the proportion of gross national product spent on higher education with a commitment to double the number of students over 25 years. That is a real attempt to have something for nothing, and it is a caricature of a weakness to which the political decision-making process in a democracy is always subject. Whatever politicians may say about 'efficiency', such a combination of proposals is necessarily a drive for the lowering of standards, and this is something which must meet academic resistance. When money is limited, quality and quantity must inevitably be alternatives.

The object of this chapter is to assert a countervailing principle, that the unit costs of higher education are a matter of academic judgement, and therefore not properly within the Government's sphere of competence. Governments may say how much money they are prepared to spend on higher education, and Universities may say, when given the sum, how many graduates that sum will buy. Between this not quite irresistible force and this not quite immovable mass, enough creative tension may build up to allow a discussion in which some healthy give and take may be possible. Each party to such a negotiation may, by listening to the other party's point of view, learn to understand what they did not before, and to distinguish the essential points of principle from those which are merely desirable.

The principle that unit costs are a matter of academic judgement follows, in the main, from the principle that teaching methods are a matter of academic judgement. This is not to say that any academic decision about teaching methods is sacrosanct: it is to say that the task of challenging it must be left to other academics. In any century, there have always been enough academics eager to please the powers that be to ensure that such people will appear to put their case to their colleagues. What is peculiar about the present situation is that at least in the rank and file of the academic profession, this urge to conciliate the powers that be has gone into abeyance perhaps more completely than in any other century in our history. Some of this, of course, is the proper result of democratic values. Some of it, however, must be seen as a result of bad politics.

Staff costs are by far the largest item in the budgets of Universities, accounting for some 75 per cent of total expenditure. This means that unit costs depend overwhelmingly on decisions about staff appointments. Such decisions raise several types of issue. They raise issues about teaching methods, about staff–student ratios, about the relationship between teaching and research time, and about the need for cover in particular subjects. All of these are matters of academic judgement.

The case for arguing that teaching methods are a matter of academic judgement has already been put.[5] It is worth adding, however, that teaching methods must be related to academic objectives. Something depends on the question, much argued in school education, how far the objective is the inculcation of information, and how far it is the teaching of a skill. To say this is not to suggest that the two objectives are antithetical or alternative. The selection of the correct context in which to place information is a skill which depends on knowledge. Yet it is possible to put the accent on one or the other. Where the accent is put may do much to influence the teaching method. The large lecture group is an effective way of purveying information. It is not labour-intensive, and it may be done reasonably cheaply. On the other hand, the development of skill is much more effectively tackled in a small tutorial group in which the teacher can engage with the student's reasoning process. It is possible to raise questions like 'What is your source for that?', and 'Does *a* really follow from *b*?' It is also, vitally, possible for the student to answer back, and argue that there are other themes which need taking into account, to which the teacher has not given sufficient weight. Indeed, the best will ask the teacher the same sort of question he asks them, including 'What is your source for that?'

It hardly needs arguing that such techniques will develop a very much more critical and independent attitude than is ever developed by listening to lectures. How much weight such points should be given is of course a matter of opinion. Yet it is a matter in which those who have not sat at both ends of a tutorial group are not entitled to an opinion: they do not have the information necessary to form one. Since so much of the information consists of atmosphere, it is very hard to convey to those not present. A transcript of a tutorial would do no more to convey the atmosphere than a transcript in Hansard can convey the atmosphere in the House, and that is not very far.

In weighing the comparative importance of skills and knowledge, much will depend on the speed at which the field is moving, and is likely to move over the next 40 years. Many graduates will have 40 years' working life in their chosen fields, and even in the most slow-moving field, a great deal changes over 40 years. This is equally true in the world outside academic life. Those living and working by the information and knowledge of 1955 would be very little use working for ICI, in the civil service, in the House of Commons, in social work or in electronics, to take only a few random examples.

What is true in these fields is equally true in academic life. If I were to repeat now the examination papers I wrote in 1958, I dread to think what mark they would be given. It is not only graduates who want to go into academic life who must be able to cope with the fact that the frontiers of knowledge are perpetually shifting. Industry, for example, must be equally in need of this quality. This is one among many reasons why supplying graduates with information alone is not a particularly useful process for the country. They must also be supplied with the skill to recognize when some of that information is discovered to have been inaccurate. Equally, they must be able to recognize which inaccuracies are merely minor adjustments, and which call a whole method or principle into question. If graduates are to justify the money invested in their production, they must understand that the frontiers of knowledge are insecurely mapped. They must be able to observe those frontiers shifting, and able to tell which of these shifts move the frontier across a watershed.

All this constitutes a strong case for the tutorial-group method of teaching. If the country cuts back on it too far, it may well not end up getting what it pays for. Even if this were the delayed consequence of the pursuit of 'efficiency' by a Government long since defeated at the polls, nothing is more certain than that Universities would be made to take the blame for it, and they must bear that risk in mind.

Equally, it provides a strong case for the union of teaching and research, a principle particularly dear to academics and a particular bugbear to Government, because it puts severe limits on any worsening of the staff–student ratio. If one of the objects is to get undergraduates to recognize that the frontiers of knowledge are mobile, no one is better qualified to demonstrate that fact than those who have themselves helped to move those frontiers, and who understand how the job is done. It is necessary to get undergraduates to understand, not merely that Professor X has proved that statement in the book isn't true, but also why his proof is convincing, and what its implications are. When I have to pull up an undergraduate for repeating a statement in one of my own books which I have subsequently refuted, I can sometimes see this generating the sort of hide-and-seek excitement which good work ought to entail. Once that lesson is learnt, it can be carried through into finding pleasure in later life in the shifting of mental horizons. It is that capacity to find pleasure in the process which makes it possible to adjust to change in later life. To paraphrase Edmund Burke, a mind that is without the means of some change is without the means of its own conservation. There is no way politicians or civil servants can quantify this sort of excitement, and no way they can ever know enough about the teaching process to judge in what forms it is best able to produce it. The case for the link between teaching and research, like other questions of teaching methods, is a matter of academic judgement, and beyond the scope of political competence. It is therefore not a proper object of Government policy. Governments have no more authority to have a policy on this question than they have to have a policy on whether the Reformation was imposed on a largely unwilling people.

Similarly, it is a matter of academic judgement in which fields appointments are needed. Again, this is not a matter in which academics are infallible. How far it is possible to understand the English Civil War without knowing about the deposition of Richard II or the madness of Henry VI is a question on which academics will disagree. It is a question the Department for Education cannot consider at all. It is, moreover, to some extent a relative question. It can be argued that all knowledge can be related to all other knowledge (given enough ingenuity) and what background knowledge any teacher finds necessary to the understanding of his subject may depend on his approach to that subject. It may be one of the advantages of a broadly-based syllabus that undergraduates will keep him on his toes by drawing background from a field with which he is unfamiliar. The question in what subjects a department requires teaching is far too complex to be prescribed to it by outside authority. Just as the Government lays down the total amount of money, and Universities decide what that money will do, so Universities may tell departments how many posts are available, and the departments must decide in what subjects those posts will be filled.

Similarly, the question across how wide a range an academic may be legitimately asked to teach is one which must be settled at the departmental level. This is not only because it depends on specialized knowledge of the academic concerned. Some of us can teach competently across a far wider range than others, and each of us is better at extending his range in some directions than in others. Knowing a colleague individually, and knowing his interests, it may be possible to judge which requests to extend his range will strike sparks of interest both from him and from his pupils, and which will merely lead to groans from one party, and yawns from the other. It must follow that the question how far the staff of a department can be reduced without making it unable to provide a proper education is one which can only be settled locally. Some departments seem to be able to run competently with three members of staff: others, in which knowledge is more specialized, seem to be unable to manage with much less than ten. The degree of specialization proper to any particular subject is something which only those in that subject can judge. Even our colleagues in other subjects are often visibly unable to assess it accurately. What is beyond the competence of academics in other subjects is *a fortiori* beyond the competence of the Department for Education.

Staffing levels, then, are a matter of academic judgement. To say this is not to write the academic community a blank cheque. In a world in which the Government determines the total level of funding, insistence on high staffing ratios in some departments will have unpleasant consequences such as the closure of others. The incentive to Universities not to have more staff than they need is very strong indeed. Indeed, it is so strong that where they say they cannot teach *x* number of students unless they have *y* number of staff, they deserve to be taken very seriously indeed. That statement, like a ministerial resignation threat, is too easily capable of backfiring to be made very lightly. For that reason, it deserves to be taken seriously when it is made. What the Government in its turn must accept is that there is a point beyond which reduction of staffing levels implies reduction of student numbers. Government must be less dogmatic in its insistence, like a sort of mirror-image Kingsley Amis, that in staffing levels less means better.

Equally, the level of library provision and laboratory equipment is necessarily a matter of academic judgement. How many copies of a particular book are needed in a College or University library is a function of how many undergraduates are going to be required to read it, and is therefore something which only teachers in that particular subject can determine. In many subjects, nothing causes more constant frustration than the practice of constantly requiring undergraduates to read books which they cannot obtain. In a bad term, undergraduates may be able to complete only half the body of required work, with obvious frustration to them, and obvious loss of academic standards. The sort of level of reading which is appropriate to undergraduates will vary between subject and subject, and between field and field within one subject. Indeed, it may vary from time to time within one field, according to the state of research in that field. When a field is stable, undergraduates may read a limited number of classic works, spiced with a flavouring of original sources, and be perfectly well prepared with a limited library provision. At other times, when a field is in a state of seismic instability, it may be necessary for undergraduates to read a much heavier diet of controversial works, especially if they are to be examined by someone whose judgement of what is significant among those controversial works will differ from that of their teacher. Indeed, the teacher himself will not know which of these books will be regarded as significant in five years' time, and since most of them will have gone out of print before the question becomes clear, he must order them all, on penalty of reducing his College's standard of education for the next twenty years if he does not. This is one reason why it is not as easy to switch the direction of a College's teaching interests as Whitehall may sometimes suppose.

Moreover, the cost of books is not under Universities' control, and rises faster than the Retail Price Index. It is with the price of books, not the Retail Price Index, that library budgets must keep pace if standards are not to decline. What is true of books is equally true of laboratory equipment. I am not capable of judging which of my scientific colleagues need an electron microscope because they cannot work without one. Only fellow scientists, and only some fellow scientists at that, can judge this question. Scientific equipment is one of the fields in which the principle that Universities are a quality market, and competition tends to drive the price up, is most clearly visible. The University with the best equipment will tend to get the best staff, and consequently the best standards, and unless the others can keep up with Professor Jones, their standard will not stay static, but fall. It is easy to see why Whitehall might deplore this process, but it is much harder to see how it could be otherwise. It is perhaps clearer in this area than in any other that unit costs are a matter of academic judgement.

Not all unit costs are a matter of academic judgement. There is an area, amounting to something under 20 per cent of costs, in which judgements on the amount which needs to be spent cannot be said to be academic ones. In this area, the question how far Universities are sovereign judges over their unit costs is not an issue of academic freedom, but of the freedom of academics. It is in this area that the questions raised by the issue of unit costs are most like those raised in the management of other public services, and in this area that answers may have the most general relevance. The principle at stake here is not that of academic freedom, but that of managerial autonomy. How far down the line can the principle of accountability be carried, and how far can the freedom of the manager to manage be combined with the right of the Government to fix spending totals? These are issues in which the position of Universities is not, in principle, different from that of, for example, British Rail.

One of the most important of these areas is that of building repair and maintenance. In University buildings, as in school and hospital buildings, this issue has become urgent because of the poor survival rate of many of the buildings put up in the 1960s. The Wilson years were the years of jerry-building, and they have been followed by the Thatcher years, which have been the years of deferred maintenance. Since the cost of building work tends to increase in geometrical progression if repairs are deferred, the case for action is strong. It should also be clear that the person in charge on the spot is the best judge of whether building repairs are needed. Whitehall may wish to scrutinize the amount of spending, but it cannot judge the likely rate of deterioration if, for example, a roof is not repaired. Only those who see where the defect is, and know the building in which it exists, are competent judges of that. The repointing of brickwork, to take one example, may in some situations be desperately urgent, while in others it may be merely a desirable operation, to be done as resources allow, but not in any sense a matter of urgency.

Yet, at the same time, Whitehall cannot be expected to write a blank cheque to authorize any building work a University officer might wish to do. Any householder knows that the amount which could be spent on perfectly defensible building work if money were no object is almost limitless. This is the sort of fact which explains Treasury fear of loss of control, and helps in understanding Treasury efforts to extend 'control' into areas in which they are very far from being competent judges. It should be said, though, that the Government's legitimate interest is in controlling the total amount spent, not on deciding that it should be spent on one particular objective. Government invocations of the principle of 'accountability' should not make them judges of whether a small sum of extra money should be spent on a new lectureship in Russian, or on replacing defective window frames. This is the sort of level of detail on which 'accountability' adds immensely to Whitehall costs (and staffing levels) without conferring any compensating benefit. If it is the University's task to judge, on grounds of managerial auto-nomy, and therefore of efficiency in its true sense, whether to spend money on window frames or on a new member of staff, then it should equally follow that it is their business to judge whether money should be spent on new window frames or on taking in additional students.

This is true, not for reasons of philosophical principle, but because it is a decision no one else is competent to make. The question is that of which is more essential to running a good University, and what con-stitutes a good University is something of which Governments are not competent judges. Universities have no right to write blank cheques for building repairs, but they do have the right to decide when expenditure on keeping out the rain is more urgent than expenditure on taking in additional students. Once again, but by a different route, we come back to the point that Universities are the only competent judges of how many students they can take for how much money. They must, of course, take such decisions in the knowledge that they have no natural right to the additional students, and that if they say they cannot do it without more money, they may be told they cannot do it at all. This is perhaps a more effective constraint on unnecessary spending than Whitehall sometimes takes it to be. Indeed, it is perhaps a more effective constraint than the exercise of 'accountability'. It is easy to make out a thoroughly convincing case for the urgency of a building repair which could in fact be put off for a couple of years, and no amount of rigorous auditing can prevent this from happening. Outside decisions on whether a building repair is necessary will necessarily include an element of the arbitrary. If, like the Ancient Mariner, they stop one of three, there is no reason for believing that the one stopped will be the least urgent.

On the other hand, institutions have a Parkinsonian urge to grow, and Universities are no exception. This urge is strongly rooted in self-interest, since with growth come preferment and promotion. With growth, perhaps more significantly, come prestige and reputation. All of us have an urge to be big, and though bigness is not actually identical with physical size, the two are very easily confused. A University which says it has a more urgent need to repoint its brickwork than to take additional students, and which says so in the knowledge that it may not gain any additional money by saying so, has a strong claim to be believed. It is, in fact, putting its money where its mouth is, and making a real sacrifice in order to do so. This again leads us back to the point that Universities are the only competent judges of their own unit costs.

What is true of building costs is, *mutatis mutandis*, normally true of other non-academic spending. It is true, for example, of expenditure on heating, lighting, telephone and postage costs. This is not to say that there is no scope for economy in such areas. Most Universities over the past twelve years have made very considerable economies on cleaning costs, and the view is sometimes expressed that they have gone too far. What is certainly true is that only those who are regularly in a building can decide whether it is adequately cleaned. The only acid test of whether more expenditure on cleaning is needed is whether people are prepared to give up something else they also want in order to get it. This is an area of managerial autonomy. The same applies to postage and telephone costs. These, however, are extremely hard to audit even on an internal level. Many University switchboards are instructed to ask, before putting a call through, 'Is this a College call?' This is a useful discipline, but it is very hard to judge the adequacy of the answers. One University has been found opening outgoing post, in order to discover whether people were abusing University free postage on private business. Here, there is an obvious conflict between the right of the University to ensure that its money is spent on University business and the right of individual members of staff to a degree of privacy. Perhaps this is an area in which it is wise to rely on a degree of mutual self-restraint.

The case for self-restraint, rather than inquisitorial auditing, applies also to lighting costs. At first sight, this may appear to be one of the areas in which scope for economy is greatest. One may often see lights on in University buildings in sunlight so bright as to recall Queen Elizabeth's objection to the candles brought by the monks of Westminster to her coronation: 'away with those tapers: we can see well enough'. Yet it turns out that to say this would be an over-simplification. Much apparently unnecessary lighting is the result of Government safety legislation, which accounts for many cases where lights are kept on in stairwells bathed in bright sunlight. This, then, in an area in which Universities' autonomy has been restricted by national legislation. Nobody disputes the right of Government to do this. In this country, though not necessarily in all, not even the most dedicated free marketeer objects to the right of the Government to regulate the market-place by legislating for safety. Whether they have done so wisely is a question for Parliament, rather than the Universities, to decide.

What does arise from this story is the question of additions to University unit costs which are the direct result of Government action. Since 1980, many of the areas in which University costs have risen faster than the Retail Price Index are the necessary consequence of actions taken by the Government. This applies, for example, to the imposition of VAT on builders' bills, one of the significant items in any University budget. The Committee of Vice-Chancellors and Principals has estimated that the increase of VAT from 15 per cent to 17.5 per cent in the 1991 budget alone added £35 million to the Universities' costs. It applies to the change in the upper limit of National Insurance. It applies to the legislation imposing higher standards on animal houses for animals used for purposes of research. I have never heard a single academic object to this legislation, and I have heard many specifically welcome it. Yet it does entail costs, and those costs have to come from somewhere. Similarly, Universities join in the move towards higher standards of access for the disabled. Yet, especially in those Universities which work in listed buildings, the costs of such access may be very considerable. On whom should these costs fall?

It may be fair, in dealing with private industry, to say that any costs arising from Government action should fall on them, and should be met, either by higher prices or by internal economies, at their managerial discretion. Imposing extra costs on industry is something Government should not do lightly, since it inevitably affects our national economic performance. Industry has every right to ask a Government which does this to think twice about what it is doing, and it deserves a hearing when it makes such a request. Yet it is fair to say that private industry has no automatic right to compensation when this happens, since it has an alternative source of funds available. It has the option of raising the money by increasing prices. Governments should think about whether they really want industry to exercise this option, but the argument against their doing so is a practical and pragmatic one: it is not sustained by any general principle save the question whether it is useful that it should do so.

Public services with an income based on charges, such as British Rail and London Underground, are a middle case. They possess the option of increasing charges, and the question whether they should exercise it is one of expediency, not of principle. Where they differ from purely private firms is the terms of reference within which the Government should consider this question. These things are normally public services because the Government wishes them to serve some public object which the market does not efficiently meet. This is often another way of saying that the costs arising from any failure in their performance will stretch beyond their own profit-and-loss accounts. For example, any decline in services provided by London Underground will show up in sharply increased road-building costs, and in the very high level of indirect costs of congestion to business in London. This has been estimated by the Confederation of British Industry at the startlingly high level of £15 billion. It is because it is almost impossible to imagine an effective market mechanism for taking these indirect costs into account that these things are best run as public services. In some cases, such as the costs of the Fennell Report on safety in the London Underground, Government chooses to meet the additional costs, rather than suffer the indirect costs of deciding not to do so. This again is a pragmatic decision, and differs from the decision in the case of private firms only in the nature of the evidence on which the pragmatic decision should be taken.

We are perhaps in a different situation in dealing with public services, such as schools, hospitals or Universities, for whom it is not in their nature to generate income from their primary functions. Universities taking in students, like hospitals taking in patients, at present offer a service whose nature is to be free at the point of delivery. There is, of course, debate in progress about how far this could or should change. If it does, it will inevitably deter demand for University education from some potential applicants, and those deterred will be selected on financial, and not academic, grounds. This debate is beside the purposes of this book. Unless or until University education ceases to be free at the point of delivery, Universities do not possess a charging mechanism to meet additional costs imposed by the Government. Under these circumstances, additional costs imposed by Government can be met, only by increased Government support or by a cut in standards or a cut in undergraduate intake. Cuts in standards, like devaluations, may in the long run weaken our international competitive position. Governments imposing additional costs on Universities, then, must be prepared either to meet them, or to let Universities contract in order to absorb them. If they deny Universities the freedom to contract, they are pursuing a policy objective, and must meet the costs of that objective. Once again, we come back to the proposition that Universities are the only competent judges of their own unit costs. Governments should not arbitrarily impose a reduction in unit costs to meet the cost of their own policies and measures.

There is a further case to be made in favour of University control over unit costs. This case is in terms of market economics. The Government, in terms of the funding of student places, is a near-monopoly buyer. It is not actually a monopoly buyer while there remain considerable numbers of high-fee overseas students, but its market share would be more than enough, in a private sector business, to justify a reference to the Monopolies and Mergers Commission. This is a position of considerable economic power. Such power is more than enough to enable the Government to enjoy a considerable leverage in achieving whatever objective it may temporarily wish to achieve. Such power must be used with restraint.

If the Government takes power to control unit costs in addition to its power as buyer, it is assuming control over both the demand and the supply. It is assuming a right to buy as much as it wants, paying whatever it wants. In such a procedure, there is no way for true costs to emerge. It is a procedure in which either there must be concealed subsidy from some other quarter, or cuts in quality must be used as a concealed subsidy underpinning a classically distorted market. While few people would argue that it is possible to have a totally undistorted market – a notion which is the latest addition to the long list of utopias – it is very hard to justify a claim that it should be distorted as much as this. If Government controls both the demand and the price, we have a classic feature of a command economy.

Such a situation is likely to lead to many of the unfortunate features of a command economy. The most obvious of those features is a tendency to produce goods which are not internationally competitive, and which are hard to sell on an international market. We do not wish to reduce British Universities to the level of East German industries, yet the application of a similar command-economy prescription will deprive us of one of the principal safeguards against such a situation, which is the process of bargaining and negotiation between demand and supply. Even outside a classic free market, that process retains a considerable value. Indeed, it is perhaps more important when a Government is in the market, rather than less important. Governments as buyers have immense power. That power, like any other power, is capable of corrupting. If it is to be used effectively and sensibly, it needs to be subject to check, and above all, needs to collide from time to time with another power. This Government is much irked by 'producer' control over the price of public services. It is precisely because this fact irks the Government so much that it is of such great value: it saves the Government from being corrupted by an excessive increase in its own power. Because it introduces a quasi-market tension into the situation, it is a pressure tending, not towards inefficiency, as the Government supposes, but towards efficiency in the true sense. It creates an opportunity to identify the true cost of the service, and thereby helps to protect it against a decline in quality.

Another familiar disadvantage of a command economy is the tendency towards corruption and the growth of a black market. This is a necessary consequence of a failure to identify true costs. If a monopoly purchaser fails to meet true costs, the service may, in a free market, disappear. If Government takes the position once expressed to me by a supporter of the Government: 'we will not *allow* Universities to close', they are denied the only legitimate response to a failure to meet their true costs. Denied a legitimate response, they would in the end become subject to an acute temptation to adopt an illegitimate response. Dealings with a University, or any other public service subjected to the same command-economy constraints, would become subject to a pressure for illegitimate gratuities. Stories were told in days gone by of the employment of staff in overseas examinations departments to extract five-pound notes from the inside of examination scripts before they reached the examiners. The sums enclosed show how old these stories are. It is perfectly possible to imagine a situation like the Soviet food-distribution business, in which, without such gratuities, the wheels simply did not turn. Indeed, the combination of a refusal to meet true costs with a prohibition of closure would, over 50 years, inevitably lead to such a consequence, because it would be the only way in which the operation could be kept going. In a command economy, corruption is one of the few ways in which the force of the market can reassert itself.

It is not, of course, inevitable that Government control over unit costs would lead to declining standards, closure or corruption. What is inevitable is that if the Government controlled unit costs, its own moderation and good sense would be our only protection against such an eventuality. It is, of course, possible to handle monopoly power with moderation, common sense and self-restraint. It has been done. In the envisaged situation of double monopoly power, as buyer and as controller of the supply, a Government might show such restraint. It would undoubtedly believe that it had done so, and that any protests to the contrary were merely self-seeking and self-interested. They might even occasionally be right in such allegations. What is true is that they would be under no restraint except such as might be voluntary and self-imposed. This is a classic definition of absolute monarchy, as well as of a command economy. In neither case has it been common for the necessary self-restraint to be kept up for very long in the absence of any built-in mechanism for securing it. Both on constitutional and on economic grounds, it is easy to argue the case that such a degree of trust should not be given to anybody. The temptation is simply too great.

To say that Universities should have control over their own unit costs is not to say they have an infinite right to public money. There is no natural right to a specified amount of public money, and Universities would remain subject to a restraint imposed by the need not to price themselves out of the market. Too high a level of unit costs would keep numbers down, or even sharply reduce them. While some Universities would no doubt survive such a process, many would not. No University would be able to know that it would be one of the successful ones. This fact would continue to impose a discipline on any temptation to impose a perfectionist level of unit costs. Moreover, a constraint would be imposed on both sides, by the existence of an international market. Though this is more true in Universities than in many other fields, it is true in many others, and it is the main reason why the idea of national sovereignty in economic matters is becoming a nostalgic memory. If it should ever become cheaper for the Government to spend public money on sending British undergraduates to Harvard and Yale than on sending them to Oxford and Cambridge, they would be perfectly free to do so. Not all undergraduates would wish to take up such an opportunity, but those who would would be quite enough to produce a dangerous reduction in demand for British University places. Undergraduates who enter University in the age range 18 to 21 are normally exceptionally free to travel, and often eager to see the world. Those doing degrees in French or German might also find that degrees from Aix en Provence or Göttingen would carry a higher prestige in the languages of those countries than British degrees can do, as well as providing an exciting chance to see the world. While poor languages will hold many British students back from taking advantage of the opportunities for mobility created by 1992, the number of Universities in the English-speaking world is quite large enough to introduce a substantial dose of healthy competition.

What is sauce for the goose is sauce for the gander, and the ability of Universities to take in overseas students is also their best protection against the near-monopoly power of their national Government. Judging by the experience already available to British Universities, German, Italian or Dutch undergraduates, to mention only a few at random, will be much less held back by inadequate languages than British undergraduates are. Many undergraduates from European countries regard the more labour-intensive British teaching system as giving British University education a quality that the Universities of their own countries lack. 1992, then, may operate in the classic way of a quality market, to drive up European University costs until they can offer an education whose quality competes with the British.

Thus, in any deadlock between British Government and British Universities international competition may be able to contribute to breaking the logjam. It certainly imposes a discipline which will help to restrain the taking of impossibly fundamentalist positions by either side. The existence of that competitive discipline is the best protection against abuse of the powers of national monopoly on either side. It is one reason for arguing that University control over unit costs will not enable them to exercise that control with the freedom they would have enjoyed in a siege economy. University power to fix unit costs, like any other power, must be used responsibly, and penalties will follow if it is not. It is only the fact that it is possible to say that with confidence which makes this position defensible.

This means that Universities must retain the sensitivity to costs which they now have, but perhaps lacked in the 1960s. There is no room for the attitude which says, in putting in a claim for public funds, 'The Government has so much: it won't feel a little sum like this.' Large sums are made up of little sums, and the cumulative effect of such an attitude, held over a long period of time, would be another Government onslaught on unit costs. The traumatic effects of this onslaught are marked deeply enough in the consciousness of Universities to make the fear that it could happen again operate like a nuclear deterrent, which gains its effectiveness from not being used rather than from being used. It is in fact a characteristic of most power that it is more effective when not used than when used. The relationship between Government and Universities is one which cannot operate without trust. When Universities appeal for that trust, they must remember that trust is a two-way process, and that their own central contribution to that trust must include not only keeping up their standards of teaching and scholarship, but also making daily efforts to avoid increases in costs. Any claim to independence from outside scrutiny must be contingent on a very high level of self-scrutiny. If that self-scrutiny should fall short, the risk that outside scrutiny might, however unjustifiably, be reimposed would return. In this area, like any other, freedom can only last if combined with responsibility. To this rule, academic freedom is no exception.

CONCLUSION

The argument that Universities know best how to manage their own business has been one of the central themes of this book. Even if such a theme can be made to stand up, it will provoke a fair and necessary question about how standards are to be preserved. Standards are not kept up automatically, and Governments may reply that they will not be kept up without external checks. It has throughout been the reply of this book to that argument that the best means of keeping up standards is competition, and that competition is ensured by the existence of an international market.

The Government may reply to that assertion by a demand to introduce a series of market mechanisms whereby competition may take place. This is unnecessary, and rests on the central free-market fallacy that competition must necessarily take an economic form. The most cursory observation of a school playground, or indeed of the House of Commons, is enough to show otherwise. The desire to win a debate is not dependent on the hope of winning the next election. It is visibly still there late at night when nothing is at stake in the vote, the cameras are off and the press has gone home. The urge to compete goes right back to the childish urge to assert that 'I said mine was bigger than yours'.

Among adults, competition for reputation is often much more intense than competition for money. Success, whether it takes the form of winning the Boat Race or of being elected a Fellow of the Royal Society, is valued as much for its addition to reputation as to income. The desire for fame, 'the last infirmity of noble mind', is often much more intense than the desire for a small competitive economic advantage, and politicians, of all professions, should be able to appreciate this fact. The number of ways in which academics can and do compete for reputation is exceptionally large, and all of these are pursued with great eagerness.

In competition among individuals, the desire to be promoted to the title of Professor does not become visibly less intense among those who have reached the top of the Reader/Senior Lecturer scale, who may obtain little or no financial advantage from their promotion. The promotion is valued as a mark of the esteem of colleagues. Other marks of this esteem are equally eagerly sought. The sensitivity of academics to the content of their reviews is notorious, and few, if any, can rise to the lofty response attributed to Joseph Conrad, that 'I don't read my reviews: I measure them.' Yet even he was searching for a quantifiable measure of other people's esteem.

The currency of reputation comes in an endless series of different forms. Invitations to write reviews for major journals, or to give papers at conferences, are current coin in this market. So, too, are invitations to give papers at major seminars, and the pride with which these things are listed by applicants for jobs or for promotion is a clear measure of the competitive value attached to them. Giving papers to such audiences, especially if they include leading scholars in the field, submits the author to a scrutiny which he will take far more seriously than he will ever take his performance on a bibliometric index compiled in Whitehall. These, like a politician's appearance on *Newsnight*, may carry no financial value whatsoever, yet the self-esteem of the scholar or politician involved may be much more heavily involved in the success of the performance than it can ever be in one for a minor audience paying a three-figure fee.

Much the same competitive sense applies to teaching. Jim Dixon (*Lucky Jim*) is not the only academic to have kept an anxious eye on the size of the intake to his special subject class. Attendance at lectures is in part a mark of status. A story is told of a famous Oxford lecturer who, as a point of one-upmanship, used to make a policy of giving his lectures at 9 a.m. on the ground that if he lectured any later, the crowd would be too big to get in. Departments watch the size of their application figures, and are quite capable of feeling a glow of one-upmanship if the department next door has places vacant at clearing house, and they do not.

Marks of reputation are the more esteemed if they are international. My father has confessed that when he was young, one of his great ambitions was to receive admiring letters from foreign scholars who knew him only through his work.[1] He is not the only academic to have formed this ambition. Reviews in foreign-language periodicals, or translations are marks of reputation, and I can remember my father showing me, with great pride, a row of his Japanese translations, of which he could not understand a word. Those who attract postgraduates from foreign countries, similarly, feel a greater sense of inner satisfaction than those who attract them only from their own. It is in the daily question 'What news on the Rialto?', in the ebb and flow of academic gossip, that this sense of competing in an international market is most obviously kept alive. It is this, not fear of losing one's job or desire to score highly on Government performance indicators, which is the spur to keep research going when the flame of curiosity burns low. It is odd that a world possessing such innumerable competitive indicators which it does respect should be thought in need of goading by a series of indicators which it does not respect. As Lady Thatcher and Mr Gorbachev have both learnt, it is respect inside one's own world which really counts.

Since the duties of academics are so multifarious, most succeed in excelling at something, and those who find teaching and research beginning to pall may usually be found competing for something else. It is not necessary to read C. P. Snow's *The Masters* to be aware that there can be intense competition for College Masterships. Posts whose duties do not primarily consist of teaching or research, like the Chairmanship of the Board of Examiners or the Deanship of the Faculty may add to the self-esteem of their holders. Any good Head of Department understands Sir John Hunt's ability, on Mount Everest, to make anyone feel they are doing the most vital job of the expedition peeling potatoes at Base Camp. It is that sense which ensures that there is always someone willing to act as Tutor for Admissions, or to provide the tea at the staff–student cricket match, and these jobs too are competitive. People will pride themselves on doing them better than anyone else.

Because academic career patterns are so individual, they are probably equipped with many more of these competitive yardsticks than most other professions. It is through these that the cultural values of the profession change when they do. Because every academic knows of the prestige which goes with catching a new research tide at the moment when it begins to flow, there is constant sensitivity to the possibility of discovering new ways of looking at things. When one is suggested, it receives instant scrutiny from people anxious to discover whether it is the tide of the future or a backwater. When the assumptions of the profession are in need of change, as all professional assumptions sometimes are, it is through this process that change will come, because it is this process that the profession has learnt to respect. All professions need to change, but they cannot be effectively changed by Government action. Even a change which might have been welcomed if it had been spontaneous risks being resisted if it is imposed by outside authority.

Attempts to change a culture by Government action create a defensive reaction which may actually retard the change in question, rather than helping it forward. Internal checks on scholarly standards, because they are so multifarious and so eagerly imposed, are far more effective than an outside scrutiny which is received with contempt because the people making it are not regarded as competent judges. Unit costs are better controlled by Government power to decide the total sum spent, or, in countries with a private University system, by what the market will bear, than they can ever be by the scrutiny of those who lack the authority to make the necessary judgements. It is odd that a profession so eager and so able to control itself should be thought to be so much in need of outside control. Even if such control could be shown to be desirable, it would remain extremely difficult to argue that it could be made effective. Universities and other professions over the centuries have usually been all too eager to comply voluntarily with the prevailing fashions, yet Lady Thatcher, like Oliver Cromwell and James II before her, has found that those who try to compel them to do so tend to lose. Yet, from the professional point of view, such victories have often tended to be Pyrrhic. On both sides, there is no practical alternative to cooperation.

EPILOGUE (APRIL 1992)

This book was written as a contribution to a debate which is now closed. The bulk of it was written during the Long Vacation of 1991, and then put aside during two very full teaching terms, the Further and Higher Education Bill, and a General Election. It thus illustrates another of the tensions in debate between political and academic values: the slow-moving character of academic change, against the fast-changing and ephemeral character of political debate. With the passage of the Further and Higher Education Act, the onset of a new funding scheme and the re-election of the Government, we have entered an entirely new round of debate, in which the issues will be different. The bulk of this book, then, is now valuable, not as a prescription for a current situation, but as an indication of the state of mind in which one academic has reached the beginning of another discussion.

During the interim period, many of the Government pressures complained of in this book have been institutionalized in the Further and Higher Education Act. They are subsequently perceived as having been ratified by the results of the General Election of April 1992. Whether that reading of the General Election is correct is a question on which it is possible to argue, but that argument is for historians: it has no political mileage. This book was written as a series of minimum negotiating positions for the restoration of trust between Universities and the State. These negotiating demands must now be regarded as having failed. The question must therefore arise whether relations between Universities and the State in Britain have reached the point of irretrievable breakdown. If they have reached that point, we must decide what we should do about it.

The new funding scheme and the Further and Higher Education Act, when taken in conjunction, have taken a very substantial further measure of academic judgement out of academics' hands. They thus constitute a further significant erosion of academic freedom. The new debate to which these changes have given rise is no longer about how trust can be restored: it cannot. The new debate will not be about negotiation with the State: it will be a debate among academics about whether the relationship with the State should be allowed to continue. Is it worth at all costs attempting to keep the show on the road, or is there a point beyond which, like a car with no brakes, it should be taken off the road whatever the consequences? It is easy to attack either decision as unacceptable, yet unless a third option can be found, one of them will have to be accepted.

The latest round of troubles began with a new scheme of research funding, in which the first key principle was that research funding was to be distributed through the research councils. Instead of going to all Universities in proportion to their student numbers, it is to go to selected Universities while the remainder are left to do without. This has been accompanied by the power to confer the title of 'University' on the former Polytechnics. That change, by itself, need not have involved any assault on academic freedom: it need only have brought the number of University places per head in Britain into line with most other countries. It is a different matter to introduce this change while destroying the link between teaching and research which was the very defining mark of Universities. The title of 'University' is to be conferred only by changing its definition. Former Polytechnics are not being given any of the rights and privileges which used to define a University: instead those rights are to be taken from some former Universities. The Government, then, has set out to change the very idea of what a University is. This is not merely moving the goalposts: it is changing rugger goalposts into hockey goalposts. It is taking away from the definition of a University the very point which, in the eyes of most academics, used to make Universities worth having. A University which does not do research is like a bicycle without wheels: one would like to know what it is for.

It has been possible for the Government to do this because, for 800 years, it has been accepted that the power to confer the title of 'University' rests in the Crown, and is exercised by Royal Charter. This power has never before been significantly abused in all the centuries it has existed. It is now being used in a way which appears as nonsensical as passing an Act of Parliament to decree that hereafter all cats shall be called 'dogs'. An institution which does not do research is not a University, and a power which attempts to decree otherwise discredits only itself. In due course, when the world has changed, this power to confer the title of 'University' must now be taken out of ministerial hands, and some checks must be placed on its exercise.

The new funding formula also includes a perpetual pressure to cut-price expansion, regardless of academic consequences. For a start, the amount of money per student is subject to a 1.5 per cent per annum 'efficiency' cut, regardless of how much inefficiency may be thereby created. Next, there is a system allowing Universities short of money (as all are) to take in additional students at cut prices, and to be rewarded the next year for having done so. There is thus a pressure for perpetual expansion regardless of academic consequences. We are told that Universities must change. Again, it seems to have become a matter for politicians, not for academics, to decide what a University shall be. Once again, the pressure on unit costs, the reduction in the amount of money *per student*, has been used as a battering ram to take academic judgement out of academic hands. This constitutes an assault on academic freedom. If academics cannot research, cannot decide how to teach, cannot defend the interests of their students, cannot decide the size of their institutions and cannot decide the standards of their degrees, what academic freedom is left to them?

It is accepted on all hands that this headlong expansion demands massive changes in teaching methods. Small groups, in which meeting of minds is possible, and students can be asked to defend their reasoning or can ask their teachers to defend theirs, are out. Massive lecture courses, suitable only for acquiring information and not for developing skills, are in. Even these are sometimes under threat: there are already cases, and will be more, in which more students have been admitted than can squeeze their way into the lecture room. Some institutions try to deal with this by teaching round the clock: I have had a conversation with one young academic, teaching from 8.30 a.m. to 10 p.m. every day, who was wondering whether to retire and become a househusband: it is not only politicians who are capable of wanting to spend more time with their families. The University of Manchester has already reported that it 'has already reached and possibly surpassed the optimum size for effective education and research'.[1] Yet if it does not expand, it will lose income. In the University of London, external examiners have already reported that some degree courses are not up to standard, and it would be a matter for surprise if there are any Universities in the country where this is not true.[2] In short, expansion without funds constitutes a continual pressure to lower the standard of the degree.

This is all the more true for the fact that, since they lost the right to Social Security benefits, many of our pupils are able to sustain themselves only by taking jobs during term. They are being asked to live at a level which the Minister of State at the Department of Social Security has already admitted is below Social Security benefit level,[3] and unless they have rich parents, jobs during term are almost unavoidable. The amount undergraduates need to survive *during term only* is now about £1,000 a year more than the combined total of grant plus loan. The point has now arrived at which applicants offered places in a University should take a year (or two if needed) to earn money before they can afford to come to University. The alternative is a second-rate education. The English three-year degree was already much shorter than any of its major competitors, and was possible only if students could do their academic work full time. There is already a sharp decline visible in the amount of academic work undergraduates are doing, and teachers have the painful decision whether to penalize them for what is not their fault. When they do have time to read, they are often unable to do so because the University has not been able to buy enough books to go round.

It is not sufficiently appreciated that this headlong drive to unfunded expansion requires an altogether new justification, and an altogether new definition, of higher education: the old ones are no longer valid. Justifications of higher education in non-vocational subjects have hitherto been offered in terms of training the mind. That involved the need for meeting of minds, and the need for careful and critical reading of books giving conflicting accounts. Both of these are now out of date. Meeting of minds requires contact with students in small groups, and critical reading of books requires enough books, and the space to store them. Neither of these things is now regularly available, and the new funding scheme guarantees that things will get worse every year. Any new justification of higher education must be cast in terms of defending the mechanical acquisition of rote learning, which is all that the new 'efficient' teaching methods can admit. In non-vocational subjects, it is hard to see what such a justification might be. If one is offered, it must of course be considered. Since none has been offered, and all the old justifications are becoming obsolete, the question must be raised whether higher education is now becoming wholly useless.

What then is left of academic freedom? In a legal sense, the right 'to put forward new ideas and controversial or unpopular opinions' still formally exists: indeed, this book is taking advantage of it now. However, even in allegedly 'research' Universities, extra people create extra business and extra crises. It is very doubtful whether even the most anti-student changes in teaching methods that can be imagined will create enough time to allow research to be done even in the most elite Universities. Even in Oxford and Cambridge, formal teaching may be taking up as much as 22 hours a week, which, after meetings, letters, reading books and so forth, is likely to add up to a 60-hour week even before any research can be attempted. Few academics will long have the dedication to make the attempt, and already people are leaving Oxford and Cambridge for the USA in order to recover the opportunity to do research. Without that opportunity, the freedom to put forward controversial or unpopular opinions becomes a bit like the sovereignty of San Marino: it cannot be effectively defended.

Beyond the formal words of Lord Jenkins' amendment, the idea of academic freedom must involve some sphere of autonomous professional judgement. There must be some things recognized as academic questions, to be decided by academics according to academic standards. It is this sphere which is now being whittled away to nothing. The words of the Jenkins amendment then become a bit like the pagan temple of Victory preserved in the Senate of Christian Rome: a sentimental reminder of departed glories. If we cannot decide how to teach, what the standard of the degree should be, what its justification and purpose are, or whether students are good enough to be admitted, what academic freedom do we have left? Professionals must have standards: without them, both grounds of self-respect and utility to society disappear. If, one after another, every one of these standards must be sacrificed on the altar of 'efficiency', what sort of professionals do we have left when the job is done? Almost everything academics are now asked to do, most of them believe to be wrong. Even if they are in error in that belief (and the possibility must be admitted), so long as they hold it, in conscience they ought to act on it. If they do not, their claim to society's respect, and indeed to their own, is forfeit. No one who has lost his professional self-respect can long remain any good at his job.

What then do we do about it? It is too late to argue that the State will see the error of its ways and relent. The State's purposes are not just those of the Conservative Party: they are shared, with almost equal determination, by Government and Opposition, because both are equally set on an expansion for which neither is prepared or able to pay. Even if we believed there would be anything worth saving in five years' time, there would be no point in waiting for the next election: any Government likely to change these policies is more than one election off.

The first question facing academics is whether battery higher education serves any useful purpose. Those who can answer 'yes' to this question may feel able to continue to serve, in the hope that some day, the spark they keep alive may be brought out and again burst into flame. Those who want to argue for this course must first explain what the useful purpose served by the expanded Universities will be, for it is only if an answer to this question can be offered that it is possible to engage in a debate with this approach. I will listen with interest to that debate when it begins, but so far, I have heard no such justification. I have heard many assert that there must be one, but I have heard no intelligible exposition of what it is.

Those who can get off the sinking ship, to America, to early retirement, or to another occupation, will presumably do so in growing numbers. This, though, gives no clue to a policy for those left in charge of what remains. What should British Universities do? So far, the main alternative policy in the field is for charging top-up fees to supplement money paid by the State. This is a high-risk strategy, and I have hitherto argued against it. A national mortgage debt of over £200 billion does not leave even many middle-class parents in a position to pay top-up fees, let alone to raise money for scholarships for those with less family money behind them. The policy of top-up fees would lead to a very small University sector, selected by parental income rather than by ability. That this would be deplorable does not need arguing. What does need arguing is whether it is better or worse than the alternative, and if the alternative were to be that higher education, as we have hitherto understood it, were not to be available to anybody, it might be better to have it available to the wrong people than to none. The policy of top-up fees, though a bad policy, is now perhaps less bad than the present situation.

The question which now needs to be answered is whether the policy of top-up fees goes far enough. The remorseless pressure from the State to whittle down the sphere of academic judgement would be slowed down rather than halted. There would be no way of preventing the State from reducing funding per student in strict proportion to the fees charged. We must then consider whether we must follow this strategy all the way, and decide, like the University of Buckingham, never to accept any money from the State. This is the only way the gentleman from Whitehall can be denied the opportunity to know best. It is, it seems, the only way any sphere of academic judgement can be preserved at all, and therefore the only way any Universities might continue to exist in Britain.

Such a strategy is very high risk indeed. The University of Buckingham has found it has to rely very heavily on overseas students: it has never achieved a large home intake. If private Universities were to achieve the quality which alone could bring in any number of students, they would be forced to charge fees approaching those of the best American Colleges, which are over 20,000 dollars a year. A British system, which has learnt over the past thirteen years to keep its costs to the bare bone, could undercut Harvard and Yale by a significant margin, but even with a loan system, it would be far beyond the reach of most British undergraduates. If the country could support two fee-paying private Universities, this would be the most that could possibly be hoped for.

The existence of one or two private Universities could make a remarkable difference to the University scene, even if they did not constitute a statistically significant proportion of it. There is a great deal to be said for competition as a means of keeping up standards. In school education, or in the health service, the existence of a private sector in competition with the State sector is a vital countervailing pressure to Government attempts to lower quality by increasing 'efficiency'. If schools, or hospitals, become too 'efficient' to be useful, middle-class voters may vote with their feet, by sending their children to independent schools or by taking out private health insurance. Similarly, nothing more clearly marks the decline of the police in public esteem than the growth of private security services. Universities are perhaps the only major service in which the State-funded sector has a total monopoly. Internationally, of course, there is no such thing, and academics are already voting with their feet in favour of the private sector in the United States. However, the flow of students abroad is likely to remain small. It is not nearly as effective a check as British private Universities, catering for students from this country, could become. The University of Buckingham already has a toehold in this market. Yet Buckingham does not have the reputation which Oxford and Cambridge, competing as private Universities, could have. If they were to offer top quality University education, regardless of price, they could confer such an advantage on their graduates in the job market that State-funded Universities would perforce be constrained to compete. The traditional British University, like the traditional British breakfast, might also sell well to foreigners. A private University, then, would be in a unique position to prevent the remorseless decline in standards which monopoly has allowed the Treasury to impose.

There would, of course, be no reason to suppose that the under-graduates recruited to such a University would be the best: they would be those from a moneyed background, and recruitment would have to be based on selection by parental bank balance, not by ability. This would, of course, be repugnant to academic values, and indeed to those of most of British society. However, the important question is not whether this would be repugnant: the answer 'yes' is all too easy. The question is whether it would be more repugnant than the alternative, and the answer to that question is not nearly so easy. If the question is whether we should have two real Universities or none, then it may be possible to argue that there is a case for the two. To the objection that they would not recruit the right people, it might be possible to reply with the (apocryphal) story of Wittgenstein on Cambridge station platform. He was deep in argument with three other people when the train started. The other three hastily clambered aboard, leaving Wittgenstein disconsolate on the platform. An old lady turned to him, and said: 'Well, at least three of you caught it.' 'Yes', said Wittgenstein, 'the three who came to see me off.' That is not a desirable result, but if the policy objective is to preserve the option of rail travel into the twenty-first century, it may just be an acceptable one. If this option preserves the ideal of University education into another century, it might, with all its disadvantages, be less objectionable than any real alternative.

Realistically, it must be admitted that this cannot be guaranteed. It is perhaps more likely that any such University would quickly go bank-rupt. However, on the premise that present Universities are becoming entirely useless, we would be no worse off if this happened than we are now. If Britain is unwilling or unable to pay for Universities at their true cost, perhaps it is better that we should face up to this fact sooner rather than later. To paraphrase Robert Jackson, it is perhaps not a bad thing that people should be made to feel the cost of their tax cuts. If people do not want Universities enough to pay for them, then they should have the courage of their convictions and do without. Whether this is because a high-quality, high-cost system could not be afforded on a mass scale, or because Universities themselves have outlived their usefulness will be a question for historians working in other countries to determine.

NOTES

INTRODUCTION

1 I owe this story to the late Sir Robert Birley, Headmaster of Eton.
2 J. S. Mill, *Essay on Liberty*, in *Essential Works of John Stuart Mill*, ed. Max Lerner (New York, 1961).
3 *Monumenta Germaniae Historica, Leges* vol. IV, p. i, ed. Ludwig Weiland (Hanover, 1893), p. 15.
4 David Willetts (*Modern Conservatism* (London, 1992) p. 21) is in error in ascribing this to something in the essence of our intellectual tradition. Until the 1981 cuts, the University vote was shared between the parties in proportions not very different from the national average.
5 *The Robbins Report* (London, 1963).
6 *House of Lords Official Report*, 19 April 1988, col. 1363.
7 ibid., 16 July 1991, cols. 103–4.
8 *Social Trends* 21 (1991), Tables 6.2 and 6.21.

1 THE IDEAL OF ACADEMIC FREEDOM

1 J. S. Mill, *Essay on Liberty*, in *Essential Works of John Stuart Mill*, ed. Max Lerner (New York, 1961), p. 273.
2 Quoted by, C. H. Lawrence, in J. I. Catto (ed.), *History of the University of Oxford*, vol. I (Oxford, 1984), pp. 98–9.
3 *History of the University of Oxford*, vol. I, p. 111.
4 ibid., pp. 1–2.
5 ibid., pp. 132, 148.
6 Beryl Smalley, *The Becket Conflict and the Schools* (Oxford, 1973), pp. 3–4.
7 ibid.
8 Elizabeth Russell, 'Marian Oxford and the Counter-Reformation', in C. M. Barron and C. Harper-Bill (eds) *The Church in Pre-Reformation Society: Essays Presented to F. R. H. Du Boulay* (Woodbridge, 1986), p. 220.
9 Bodleian Library, MS Clarendon, vol. 20, no. 1528.
10 *House of Lords Official Report*, 28 June 1988, col. 1395.
11 ibid., col. 1406.
12 Mill, *On Liberty*, p. 277.
13 *House of Lords Official Report*, 19 April 1988, col. 1408.

14 Lord Swann, 'The Law, Freedom and the Middle Ground', lecture given at St George's House, Windsor, on 20 April 1990. I would like to thank the late Lord Swann for a typescript of this lecture.
15 Law Report, *The Independent*, 30 August 1991.
16 *House of Lords Official Report*, 19 May 1988, col. 485.
17 Bertrand Russell, *Autobiography*, vol. I (London, 1967), p. 152.
18 *The Independent Magazine*, 14 September 1991.
19 Lord Swann, 'The Law, Freedom and the Middle Ground', p. 12.
20 Lord Swann, 'The Law, Freedom and the Middle Ground', pp. 4–5.
21 John Aubrey, *Brief Lives*, ed. Oliver Lawson Dick (London, 1949), pp. 114, 112; also Public Record Office, S.O. 3/12, folio 117v.
22 Conrad Russell, *The Crisis of Parliaments* (Oxford, 1971), p. 182.
23 *The Independent*, 20 August 1991.
24 Mill, *On Liberty*, p. 356.
25 *House of Lords Official Report*, 19 April 1988, col. 1407.

2 THE LIMITS OF ACADEMIC FREEDOM

1 J. S. Mill, *Essay on Liberty*, in *Essential Works of John Stuart Mill*, ed. Max Lerner (New York, 1961), p. 304.
2 Article 25 of the Act of Union of 1707, quoted by Lord Grimond, *House of Lords Official Report*, 16 May 1988, col. 135.
3 *House of Lords Official Report*, 25 July 1988, col. 33.
4 ibid., 28 June 1988, cols 1429 and 1430–9.
5 *House of Commons Employment Committee, Minutes of Evidence*, 6 March 1991, Questions 33–5.
6 *Times Higher Education Supplement*, 2 December 1988.
7 *House of Lords Official Report*, 28 June 1988, col. 1399.
8 ibid., col. 1402.
9 J. I. Catto (ed.), *History of the University of Oxford*, vol. I (Oxford, 1984), pp. 131–2.

3 MAPPING THE BORDERS

1 Hansard, 26 July 1967, col. 749.
2 Quoted by Lord Wedderburn of Charlton, *House of Lords Official Report*, 18 April 1988, col. 1342.
3 ibid., 3 May 1989, col. 239.
4 Bertrand Russell, *Autobiography* vol. II, (London, 1968) p. 103.
5 This statement is based on personal knowledge up to 1984. Occasional conversations suggest a faint doubt as to how far it is still true.
6 I owe this information to an unpublished paper by Professor C. H. Lawrence.
7 Elizabeth Russell, 'Marian Oxford and the Counter-Reformation', in C. M. Barron and C. Harper-Bill, eds, *The Church in Pre-Reformation Society: Essays Presented to F. R. H. Du Boulay* (Woodbridge, 1986), p. 224.
8 Personal communication: the example is not imaginary.
9 *House of Lords Official Report*, 15 May 1991, col. 1704. (Debate on the abolition of the vacation hardship allowance.)
10 ibid., 28 June 1990, col. 1790.

10 ibid., 28 June 1990, col. 1790.
11 ibid., 28 June 1988, col. 1407.
12 ibid., 17 October 1988, col. 956.
13 ibid., col. 954.

4 UNIT COSTS

1 Hansard, 17 May 1989, col. 328.
2 *House of Lords Official Report*, 15 June 1989, col. 1515.
3 *The Independent*, 6 September 1991.
4 *House of Lords Official Report*, 19 May 1988, col. 471.
5 See Ch. 3, pp. 72–3.

CONCLUSION

1 Bertrand Russell, *Autobiography*, vol. I, (London, 1967) p. 133.

EPILOGUE

1 *The Independent*, 23 December 1991.
2 *The Independent*, 23 March 1992.
3 Letter from Rt. Hon. Nicholas Scott PC MP, 20 April 1990, quoted in *House of Lords Official Report*, 21 May 1990, col. 650.

INDEX

117

Richelieu, Cardinal 34
Robbins Report (1963) 5,6
Russell, Bertrand 24,37,60,102
Russian 75–6

St Andrews, University of 46
Scott, Rt.Hon. Nicholas, MP 107–8
Selden, John 9
Ship Money, Case of (1637–8) 18–19
social sciences 32–4,75,81
Social Security benefits, student loss
   of entitlement to 107–8
Socrates 78
Soviet Union, former 60,98
staff costs 86–7
staffing levels 90
Stamford, alleged University of 55–6
Steel, Rt.Hon. Sir David, MP 6
subjects, balance of 74–6
Swann, Lord 27
Swinnerton-Dyer, Sir Peter 50,59

teaching and research, union of
   28,88–9
teaching methods 72–3,87–91,107
tenure 20,22–7,43
Triplet, Thomas 18

Union, Act of (1707) 46–7
University College, London 18
University costs 13
University education, objectives of
   87,107,108–112
University Grants Committee,
   former 50,52
University, title of, power to confer
   106

vacations, use of 68–9,73–4
Vice-Chancellors 12,80

Wooding Report 75–6

Yeltsin, Boris 35